Old Town School of Folk Music SONGBOOK

Edited by Michael J. Miles and Jimmy Tomasello
Arrangements by Michael J. Miles

ISBN-13: 978-1-4234-1846-7

HAL•LEONARD® CORPORATION

7777 W. BLUEMOUND RD. P.O. BOX 13819 MILWAUKEE, WI 53213

Visit Hal Leonard Online at
www.halleonard.com

In Australia Contact:
Hal Leonard Australia Pty. Ltd.
4 Lentara Court
Cheltenham, Victoria, 3192 Australia
Email: ausadmin@halleonard.com

CONTENTS

Cover: (From left) Big Bill Broonzy, Frank Hamilton and Win Stracke on Opening Night, 1957.

WHAT IS THE OLD TOWN SCHOOL OF FOLK MUSIC?

WIN STRACKE TOLD THE STORY OF THE OLD TOWN SCHOOL OF FOLK MUSIC BACK IN 1967, AND HIS WORDS ARE STILL THE BEST DESCRIPTION OF THE SCHOOLS HISTORY ANYWHERE. THIS ESSAY IS EXCERPTED FROM WIN'S PAMPHLET, "THE BIOGRAPHY OF A HUNCH."

WIN'S HUNCH. All of this got started because of a hunch I had, back in 1957. Early in the spring of that year, I was doing a three-week stint at the old Gate of Horn, the folksong nightclub at Chicago and Dearborn. Along about that time, I met two people who were going to be really important in everything that happened later. One was a young unknown folk musician who arrived at the club to accompany one of the performers. The other was an Oak Park housewife who had become a serious fan of the growing folk music scene.

The musician was Frank Hamilton. When he arrived at "The Gate," he amazed just about everybody with his facility on different folk instruments, his creative improvisational ability, and the playful joyousness that he brought to any kind of traditional music.

The housewife was Dawn Greening, a woman with enough generosity, enthusiasm, taste, and love of folk music for five people. She knew Frank needed an income, that he was a gifted teacher, and that he had picked up some innovative techniques from Bess Lomax Hawes on the West Coast. So Dawn and her husband Nate made a space in the Greening dining room for Frank to hold weekly classes. I attended one of those classes with 14 others, and it was there the hunch was born.

One night, about three weeks into those classes, as I was driving Frank home, I put the idea to him. I suggested that we could organize a school around him and his teaching techniques— a school in which he would use the same dining room approach but for larger classes. We talked about how it would work. Frank agreed, and the project was on.

A word about my hunch is in order. There was no doubt in my mind that there was a growing demand for good teaching of folk music. During my career on TV, I'd been getting hundreds of requests from parents to teach guitar to their children, but I knew that if a performer took on a full schedule of teaching individual students, he or she usually stopped being a successful singer. The way out of this dilemma was class lessons, especially the way Frank taught them. And this also happened to be a great way for people to learn how to play guitar.

Using my studio in the old Immigrant State Bank Building on North Avenue as an office, I enlisted the aid of my friend and neighbor, Gertrude Soltker, to help organize the school. Press releases were prepared, announcements were made over WFMT, and a registration day was set.

OPENING NIGHT, DECEMBER 1ST, 1957. The opening ceremonies and registration on December 1, 1957, were a smash. Several hundred prospective students attended, along with a fine representation of performers, educators, and Old Town notables. George Armstrong opened the proceedings with the strains of the bagpipes; Frank Hamilton gave a demonstration of his teaching method, using our former Oak Park group as guinea pigs; Big Bill Broonzy performed one of his blues numbers and, on the spot, Frank analyzed and reproduced Bill's intricate right-hand style in written tablature on a blackboard and then played back an exact rendition

Opening night of classes at the Old Town School of Folk Music, December 1, 1957. Left to right: Frank Hamilton, George Armstrong, Win Stracke.

of Bill's playing. That night we also instituted the coffee break that has continued to be a part of every Old Town School class. We closed the evening with a songfest, and the School was on its way.

The School expanded and, by its second year, held classes on Tuesday and Thursday evenings and Saturday afternoons.

One of the reasons that the School was so successful was that it was also a gratifying social experience. From the beginning, students were encouraged to help each other. The coffee break added to the social atmosphere, and the "second half," with all the students singing and playing at their own level, has continued.

And the composition of the student body has always provided an interesting chemistry. In our classes you'll find just about everything: engineers and office workers, housewives and hockey players, brokers and bus drivers, priests and psychiatrists, firemen and photographers. At the same time we were lucky from the beginning to have the enthusiastic and generous support of the professional folksinging community. If I were to start listing the singers and folklorists who have performed at the school without compensation - names like Pete Seeger, Odetta, Studs Terkel, Doc Watson, Mahalia Jackson, Bill Monroe, the Weavers, Jean Ritchie - it would take a long time to reach the end of the list.

A word about our teachers. Many of them learned their skills here and stayed on to become part of the teaching staff. Many more were fine performers who wanted to become part of the

school. All of them have been dedicated, loyal, and enthusiastic. The school and they have grown together.

Many thousands of students have by now attended classes. And while the school has always insisted that its main purpose was to give performing skills to amateurs - in the best sense of that word - some of these students became performers: people like Steve Goodman, John Prine, Jim McGuinn, Ginni Clemmens, Valucha, and Fred and Ed Holstein.

When we opened our doors on December 1, 1957, we described ourselves, in what now seems a burst of overconfindence, as "America's first permanent school for the study of folk music and folk instruments." Somehow we have tapped the strength, the beauty, the longevity of the songs we sing and channeled these qualities into a gathering place we call the Old Town School of Folk Music. We have built an institution that commands nationwide respect. It seems the hunch was right!

(Win Stracke died in 1991. The School set up a scholarship fund in honor of his efforts to expose people from all backgrounds to the joy of music.)

THE OLD TOWN SCHOOL OF FOLK MUSIC
50TH ANNIVERSARY SONGBOOK
FOLKSINGER AND SONGWRITER MARK DVORAK, A MEMBER OF THE OLD TOWN SCHOOL OF FOLK MUSIC'S FACULTY SINCE 1986, TELLS THE STORY OF OUR SONGBOOK IN 2007.

Some time ago, a former student gave me a copy of the original Old Town School of Folk Music songbook as a gift. Though the Old Town School opened in 1957, I don't think the first songbook appeared until about a year later. There's no copyright page in mine, so it's hard to tell; I suppose someone somewhere knows. Whenever it came to be, I'm told it was created by Win Stracke, the school's first director, and Frank Hamilton, the first instructor. It seems almost inconceivable that anyone would think of starting up a music school without a songbook. But that's the way Win and Frank wanted to do it.

Win and Frank loved music of all kinds. Win was a trained singer with a deep bass voice. He sang folk songs his whole life but also sang in classical settings, choirs, and even an opera or two. He enjoyed a successful career in radio and television and at one time was quite the celebrity. Frank grew up in Los Angeles and was remarkably young when he and Win opened the School. He was skilled on several instruments and was already an accomplished folk and jazz musician. Frank was also a talented teacher of folk music classes, having learned firsthand from a woman named Bess Lomax Hawes in California.

Both Frank and Win had a great knowledge of — and deep respect for — folk songs from many countries. Together they envisioned a school where people could not only celebrate the American tradition of song and dance, but could also become acquainted with the musical traditions of different world cultures. Their new school would be a meeting-house for musicians, storytellers, folk dancers, folklorists and professional entertainers who would gather to share their knowledge and experience with the public.

They fashioned a curriculum and developed a teaching technique. Hailed as "innovative" at the time, Frank and Win's creative new approach to learning music was actually based upon the age old methods folks have always used: listening, watching, trial and error and playing by ear. When they finally did get around to assembling the original "textbook" as it was called, it was done only after considerable discussion and debate.

Win and Frank wanted their book to be easy for students to use. It had to be inexpensive to produce. They wanted it to be representative of the North American folk song tradition. They wanted songs from other countries to be included. The songs had to be simple. They favored lots of songs that were suitable for group involvement. Where other music schools taught theory and performance, Win and Frank wanted the Old Town School "method" to retain its emphasis on participation and development of aural skills.

Finally, 94 songs were settled upon. Most were North American folk songs, but selections from Israel, Ireland, England, Chile, and a Cajun love song were added. Each page gave a sentence or two of background about the song while the chord progression and rhythm indicators were printed above the verses. Chord fingering charts for guitar, and in some cases banjo, were pictured, and at the bottom of each page the melody was written out in standard music notation.

Frank Hamilton and Win Stracke.

The book was issued to students unbound. The pages were 3-hole punched and to be put in a ring binder. The intention here was for all students to start out with the same collection of songs. As handouts from different classes were added to the binder, no two books — or no two students — might evolve identically.

This new 50th Anniversary edition is the sixth or seventh, depending on whom you ask, and it's a whole lot different than the original. There are now 117 songs in all — two dozen of which are half-century survivors from Win and Frank's original selection. The information appendix has also been updated and expanded to include reference material on the most popular folk instruments studied at the Old Town School. It is chock-full of clearly presented, useful information.

What a treasure is the new Old Town School of Folk Music Songbook! Some of the sturdiest songs known to the English-speaking world — from centuries-old ballads to African-American spirituals to old¬timey numbers to blues to folk favorites to songs from Chicago's own rich songwriting tradition — are all bound together in a single collection. Each song is a doorway through which lies an opportunity to renew ourselves; to discover again what remains common in our long and varied musical heritage.

In a way, every musician and songwriter is a kind of folklorist. We ask questions. In what we learn from people and books and recordings we sometimes find answers. Which lead to more questions. Throughout our musical lives, we review our growing catalogues of truth and sort through our expanding inventories of things unknown. Piece by piece, a personal collection of sounds, images and experiences is somewhere being assembled in our minds and hearts. That collection contains the real stuff out of which real music is made. And with practice comes the promise that our music will one day reveal a beautiful reflection of who we are and from where we've come.

For certain, there is no shortage of virtuosos in our musical world. Performances and recordings abound that remind us that indeed, some are born with extraordinary gifts. But I hope in learning the songs in the 50th Anniversary Old Town School of Folk Music Songbook, singers and musicians will also learn that, for a long time now, folks with ordinary gifts have been responding musically to the world around them in extraordinary ways. That's an idea I now think Win and Frank must have known a whole lot about by the time they opened the Old Town School of Folk Music.

Mark Dvorak
Chicago, IL
April 2007

After The Ball

Charles K. Harris

AFTER THE BALL (additional verses)

"Bright lights were flashing in the grand ballroom,
Softly the music playing sweet tunes.
There came my sweetheart, my love, my own,
'I wish some water; leave me alone.'
When I returned, dear, there stood a man
Kissing my sweetheart as lovers can.
Down fell the glass, pet, broken, that's all—
Just as my heart was after the ball."

"Long years have passed, child, I have never wed,
True to my lost love though she is dead.
She tried to tell me, tried to explain—
I would not listen, pleadings were vain.
One day a letter came from that man;
He was her brother, the letter ran.
That's why I'm lonely, no home at all—
I broke her heart, pct, after the ball."

Old Town School of Folk Music

Amazing Grace

Traditional

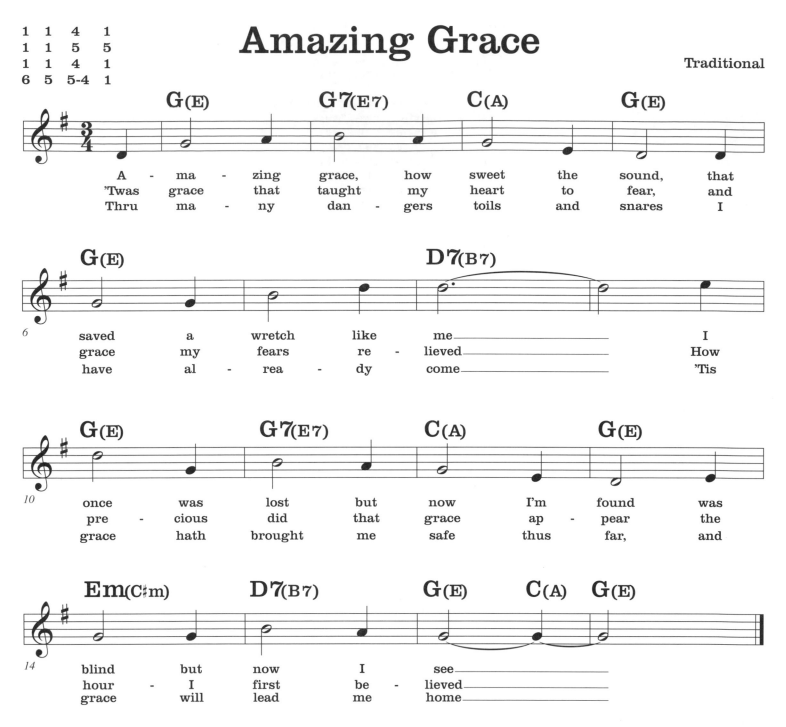

How sweet the name of Jesus sounds
In a believer's ear
It soothes his sorrows, heal his wounds
And drives away his fear

Angel Band

Traditional

Aragon Mill

Si Kahn

Old Town School of Folk Music

At The Old Second Half

Robbie Fulks

In the pale gleam of eve - ning a gen - tle voice says, Sim - ple
Chorus: Let us go let us ga - ther when class time is o'er, Spread in

words old and dear that my heart che - rish - es, Nine o -
sweet con - gre - ga - tion 'cross the old school - house floor. There to

clock get thee hi - ther to join the mer - ry staff, of the
join in sweet des - cant to drink per - chance to laugh, los - ing

school of folk mu - sic at the old se - cond half
heart's care in cho - rus at the old se - cond half

To the pounding bass viol, we sing a roundelay
Ever watchful sweet spirs of a long bygone day
To our forebears in folklore, we raise high the carafe
'Tis a small step from stupor at The Old Second Half

Ne'er an alehouse in London, nor a Paris cafe
To the heart grants such rapture, knows a pageant so gay
Dance we on then, like madmen, and for an epitaph
"May (his) soul rest contented in the Great Second Half."

Old Town School of Folk Music

Aunt Rhody

Traditional

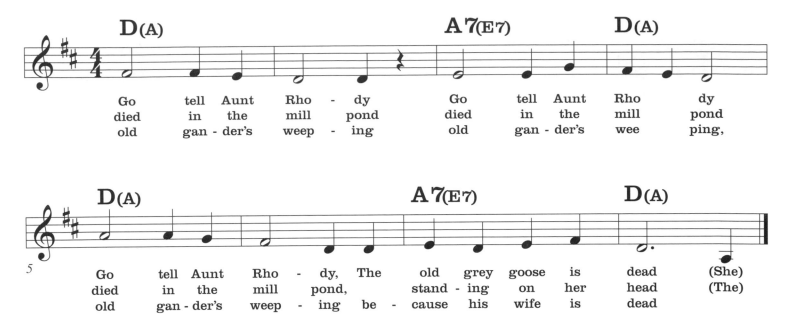

Go tell Aunt Rho - dy Go tell Aunt Rho - dy
died in the mill pond died in the mill pond
old gan - der's weep - ing old gan - der's wee ping,

Go tell Aunt Rho - dy, The old grey goose is dead (She)
died in the mill pond, The
old gan - der's weep - ing be - cause his wife is dead

standing on her head
old stand - ing on her head dead
(The)

Old Town School of Folk Music

1155
5511
1144
1511

Banks Of The Ohio

Traditional

I asked my love to take a walk just to
CHORUS: Then on - ly say that you'll be mine and in

go a lit - tle way Down be -
no o - thers arms you'll twine Down be -

low where the wa - ters flow, down by the
side where the wa - ters flow down by the

banks of the O - hi - o
banks of the O - hi - o

I drew a sword across her breast
As gently in my arms she pressed
Crying, "Willie, don't murder me.
I'm unprepared for eternity."

I took her by her lily white hand
Led her down where the water stands
I picked her up and I threw her in
And watched her as she floated down

I started home about half past one
Crying, "Lord what have I done?"
Murdered the only girl I loved
Because she would not marry me

Old Town School of Folk Music

Bill Bailey

Traditional

Blow Ye Winds

Traditional

D

Tis ad - ver - tised in Bos - ton New York and Buf - a lo Five
They send you to New Bed - ford that fam - ous wha - ling port, And
They send you to a board - ing house there for a time to dwell, The

G   **D**   **A**

hun - dred brave A - mer - i - cans a - wha - ling for to go Sing - ing
give to you some land-sharks for to board and fit you out Sing - ing
thieves they there are thick - er than the o - ther side of hell, Sing - ing

D   **D**

Blow ye winds in the morn - ing Blow ye winds high ho!

G   **D**   **A**   **D**

Clear a - way your run - ning gear and blow ye winds high - O!

It's now we're out to sea my boys
The wind comes on to blow
One half the watch is sick on deck
The other half below

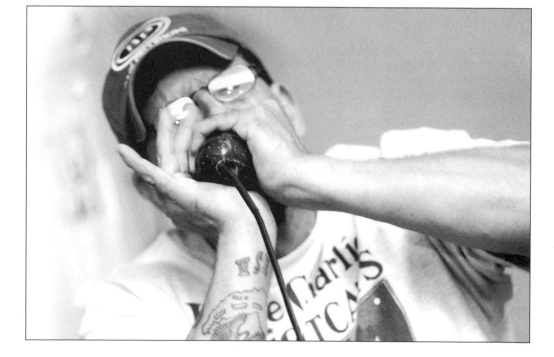

Old Town School of Folk Music

Boil Them Cabbage Down

Traditional

```
1  4  1    5
1  4  1-5  1
```

Boil them cab-bage down boys, Turn them hoe cakes round. The
on-ly song that I could sing was boil them cab-bage down.

Went up on the moun-tain just to give my horn a blow,
Took my gal to the black-smith shop, to have her mouth made small
Some-one stole my old 'coon dog—— Wish they'd bring him back

Thought I heard my true love say, "Yon-der comes my beau."
She turned 'round a time or two and swal-lowed shop and all.
Chased the big ones through the fence, and the little ones thru the crack.

Met a possum in the road
Blind as he could be
Jumped the fence and whipped my dog
And bristled up at me.

Once I had an old gray mule
His name was Simon Slick
Hed roll his eyes and back his ears
And how that mule would kick

How that mule would kick
He kicked with his dying breath
He shoved his hind feet down his throat
And kicked himself to death.

Brown's Ferry Blues

Traditional

Buffalo Gals

Traditional

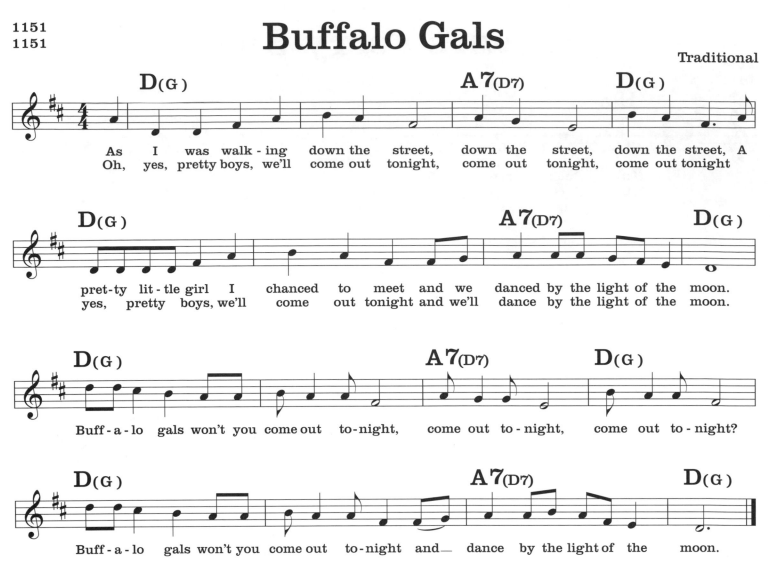

Dance with the dolly with the hole in her stocking
While her knees keep a knocking and her toes keep a rocking
Dance with the dolly with the hole in her stocking
And we'll dance by the light of the moon.

Old Town School of Folk Music

1155
1151
1141
1151

Camptown Races

Stephen Foster

C(G) .... G7(D7)

Camp - town la - dies sing this song,
Long - tail filly and big black horse } Doo - dah Doo - dah
Come down south with your hat caved in }

C(G) .... G7(D7) C(G)

Camp - town race is five miles long,
Come to a mud hole they all cut across } Oh the doo - dah day.
Go back north with a pocket full of tin }

C(G) .... F(C) C(G)

Goin' to run all night, Goin' to run all day. I

C(G) .... G7(D7) C(G)

bet my mo - ney on the bob - tail nag. Some - bo - dy bet on the bay

Old Town School of Folk Music

Careless Love

Traditional

Cat Came Back

Traditional

Old Town School of Folk Music

1 1 1 5
1 4 5 1
4 4 1 1
4 4 5 1

Cindy

Traditional

Oh   have you seen my   Cin - dy,   she   comes from way down   south.
I   wish I   was   an   ap - ple   just   hang - in'   in   a   tree
She   told   me   that she   loved me.   She   called me   "Su - gar   Plum,"   She

she's so sweet the   ho - ney bees just   swarm a - round her   mouth. Get a-long
Ev - 'ry time my   sweet-heart passed she'd   take   a   bite of   me
threw her arms a -   round me   and   I   thought my   time had   come.

home   Cin - dy   Cin - dy,   Get a-long   home,   Get a-long

home   Cin - dy   Cin - dy   I'll   mar - ry   you   some   day.

She took me to the parlor.
She cooled me with her fan.
She swore I was the purtiest thing
In the shape of a mortal man

Oh Cindy got religion
She had it once before
But when she heard my old banjo
She was the first one on the floor.

Old Town School of Folk Music

CC Rider

Traditional

1111
4411
5515

C   C Rider —— see what —— you have done

C   C Rider see what —— you have done

Oh you made ——

— me love —— you ——   now your man has   come

I'm goin' I'm goin' and your cryin' won't make me stay
I'm goin' I'm goin' and your cryin' won't make me stay
The more you cry baby, the further you drive me away

I told you woman, I'll tell your partner too
I told you woman, I'll tell your partner too
That your three times seven, you know what to do

I'd rather drink muddy water and sleep in a hollow log
I'd rather drink muddy water and sleep in a hollow log
Than to live in Chicago and get treated like a dog

Old Town School of Folk Music

City Of New Orleans

Steve Goodman

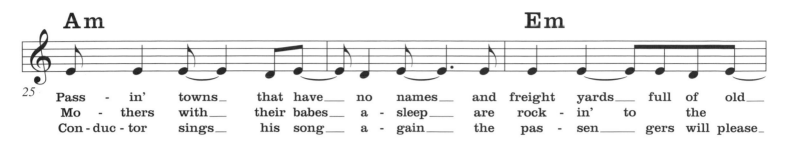

Am   Em

Pass - in' towns___ that have___ no names___ and freight yards___ full of old___
Mo - thers with___ their babes___ a - sleep___ are rock - in' to the
Con - duc - tor sings___ his song___ a - gain___ the pas - sen___ gers will please

G   G7

___ black men___ and the grave yards___ of the rust - ed au - to mo - biles___
gen - tle beat___ and the rhy - thm___ of the rails is all___ they feel
___ re - frain___ this train's got the dis - ap - pear - in' rail road___ blues

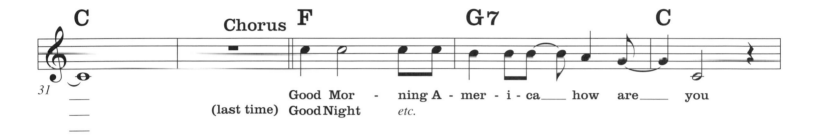

C   Chorus F   G7   C

___   Good Mor - ning A - mer - i - ca___ how are___ you
___ (last time) Good Night *etc.*
___

Am   F   C

Say, don't you know___ me I'm your na - tive son

G7 C   G7   Am

I'm the train they call the Ci - ty of___ New Or___ leans

F   G7   C   C

I'll be gone five hun - dred miles___ when the day___ is done.

Old Town School of Folk Music

Colorado Trail

Traditional

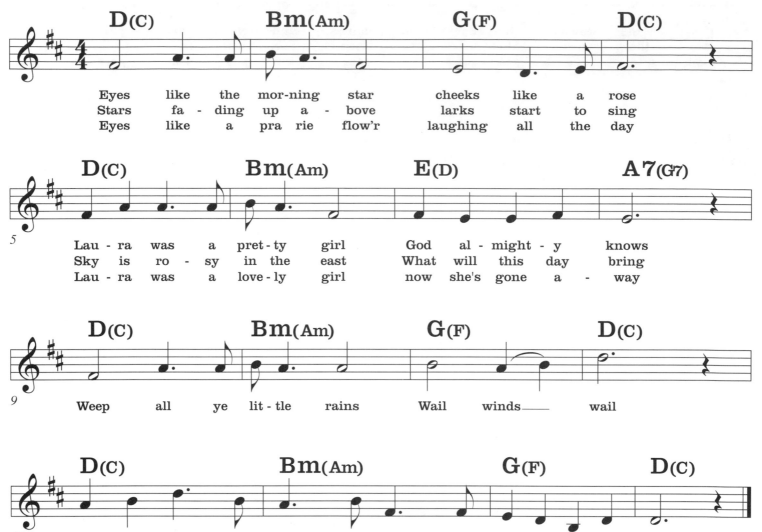

Eyes like the mor-ning star cheeks like a rose
Stars fa - ding up a - bove larks start to sing
Eyes like a pra rie flow'r laughing all the day

Lau - ra was a pret-ty girl God al - might - y knows
Sky is ro - sy in the east What will this day bring
Lau - ra was a love-ly girl now she's gone a - way

Weep all ye lit - tle rains Wail winds——— wail

All a - long a - long a - long the Co - lo - ra - do trail

Old Town School of Folk Music

Corinna, Corinna

1111
4411
5511

Traditional

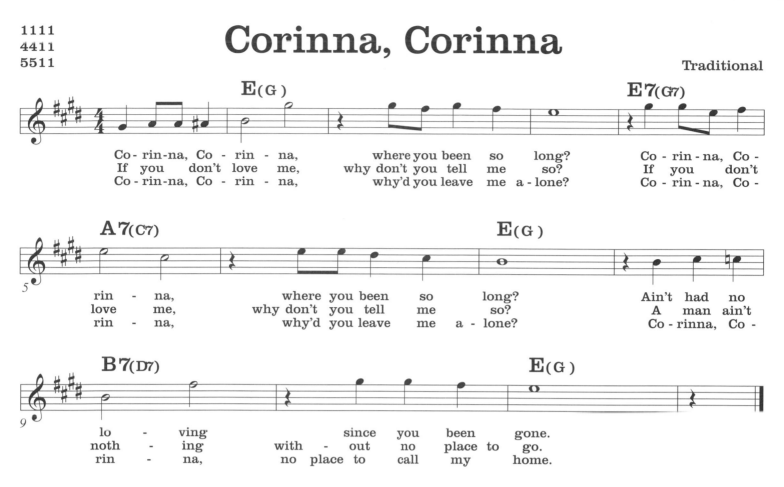

E(G)

Co - rin-na, Co - rin - na,   where you been   so   long?   Co - rin - na, Co -
If you   don't love   me,   why don't you tell   me   so?   If you   don't
Co - rin-na, Co - rin - na,   why'd you leave   me a - lone?   Co - rin - na, Co -

A7(C7)   E(G)

rin - na,   where you been   so   long?   Ain't had no
love   me,   why don't you tell   me   so?   A man ain't
rin - na,   why'd you leave   me a - lone?   Co - rinna, Co -

B7(D7)   E(G)

lo - ving   since you been   gone.
noth - ing   with - out no   place to   go.
rin - na,   no place to   call   my   home.

Got a bird that whistles, got a bird that sings
Got a bird that whistles, got a bird that sings
Without Corinna, it don't mean a thing

Old Town School of Folk Music

Crawdad Song

Traditional

1111
1155
1144
1511

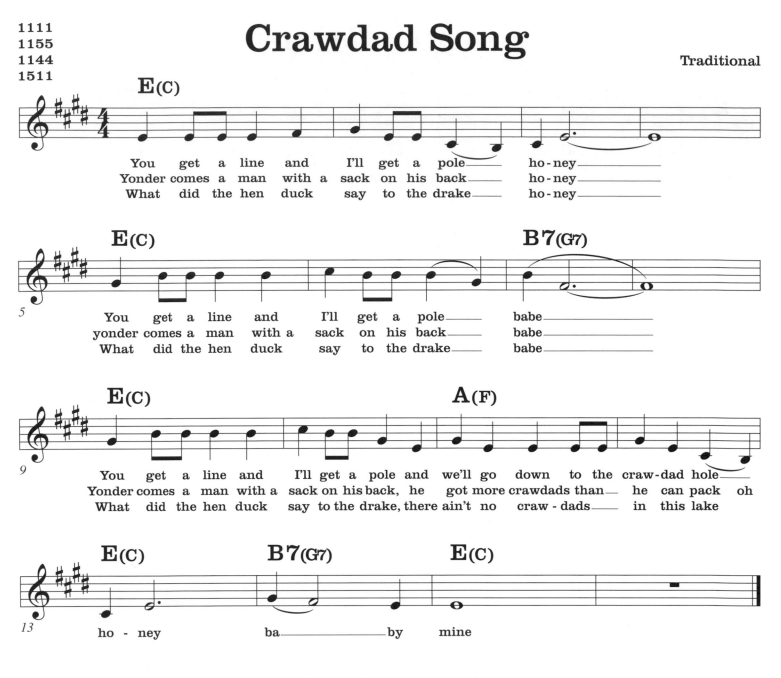

E(C)

You get a line and I'll get a pole——— ho-ney———
Yonder comes a man with a sack on his back——— ho-ney———
What did the hen duck say to the drake——— ho-ney———

E(C) — **B7(G7)**

You get a line and I'll get a pole——— babe———
yonder comes a man with a sack on his back——— babe———
What did the hen duck say to the drake——— babe———

E(C) — **A(F)**

You get a line and I'll get a pole and we'll go down to the craw-dad hole———
Yonder comes a man with a sack on his back, he got more crawdads than— he can pack oh
What did the hen duck say to the drake, there ain't no craw-dads——— in this lake

E(C) — **B7(G7)** — **E(C)**

ho - ney ba———by mine

What'ya gonna do when the lake runs dry honey
What'ya gonna do when the lake runs dry babe
What'ya donna do when the lake runs dry
Just sit on the bank and watch the crawdads die
Honey baby mine

Crawdads live and crawdads die, honey
Crawdads live and crawdads die, babe
Crawdads live and crawdads die
Ain't no reason to wonder why
Honey baby mine

Apple cider cinnamon beer, honey
Apple cider cinnamon beer, babe
Apple cider cinnamon beer,
Cold hog's head and a possum's ear
Honey, baby, mine.

Old Town School of Folk Music

Cripple Creek

Traditional

Cross Road Blues

Robert Johnson

1411
4411
5511

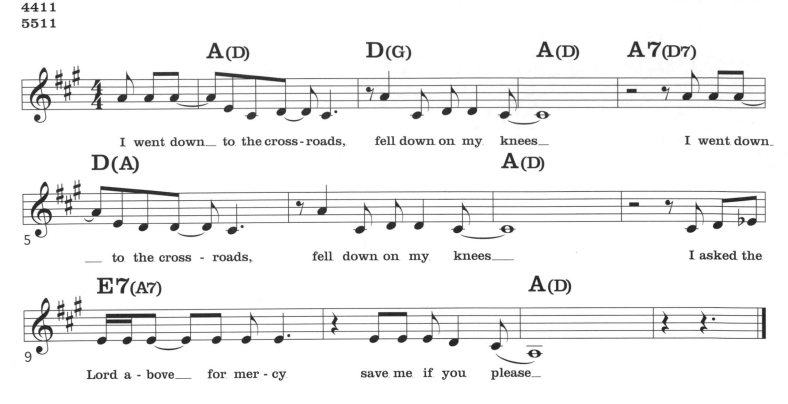

I went down to the cross-roads, fell down on my knees I went down to the cross-roads, fell down on my knees I asked the Lord a-bove for mer-cy save me if you please

I'm goin' down to Rosedale, got my rider by my side
I'm goin' down to Rosedale, got my rider by my side
You can still barrel-house baby, by the riverside

You can run, you can run, tell my friend boy Willie Brown
You can run, you can run, tell my friend boy Willie Brown
Standin' at the crossroads, believe I'm sinkin' down

I went to the crossroads, I looked east and west
I went to the crossroads, I looked east and west
I didn't have no woman, oh well, in my distress

Old Town School of Folk Music

Deep River Blues

Traditional

Delicate Balance

Tom Dundee

I dreamed I was barer than naked
It scared me so bad that I called,
"Help me back to the prison
with the chains of the living!"
Although nothing had hurt me at all

And it's all such a delicate balance
As it turns throught he circles of air
To worry does nothing
But steals from the loving
And robs from the pleasure that's there.

Deep within there's a feeling
Love and understanding is the door
Honesty is the key
That was given you and me
To open it and so many more

And it's all such a delicate balance
It takes away as much as it give
But to live it is real
And to love is to feel
You're a part of what everything is

1411
6645
641511

Dink's Song

Traditional

If I had wings like No-ah's dove,
I've got a man and he's long and tall
Re-member one night, a driz-zlin' rain,

I'd fly up the
he moves his bo-
you'll call my

ri - ver to the one I love.
dy like a can - non - ball
name and I'll be gone.

Fare thee

well oh hon-ey fare thee well.

Remember one night, a drizzlin' rain,
'Round my heart I felt a pain.
Fare thee well, oh honey, fare thee well.

Don't This Road Look Rough & Rocky

Traditional

Dar - ling, I have come to tell you,
Don't you hear the night birds cry - ing
One more kiss be - fore I leave you,

though it al - most breaks my heart,
on some dark and lone - ly sea,
One more kiss be - fore we part.

that be - fore the mor - ning
while of o - thers you are
You have caused me lots of

dar - ling, we'll be ma - ny miles a - part
think - ing, won't you some-times think of me?
trou - ble, dar - ling you have broke my heart.

Chorus:

Don't this road look rough and rock - y? Don't that sea look wide and deep?

Don't my ba - by look the sweet - est when she's in my arms a - sleep

Old Town School of Folk Music

Don't You Hear Jerusalem Moan?

Traditional

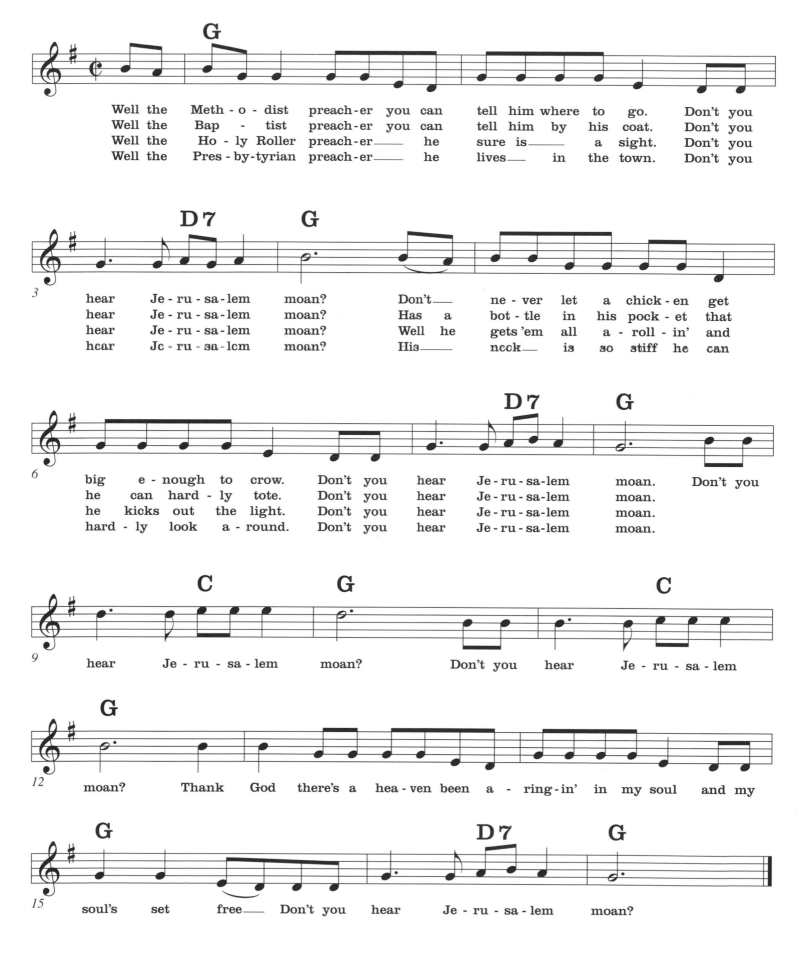

Old Town School of Folk Music

1111
1141
1111
2511

Done Laid Around

Traditional

Done hung around and sung around this old town all year.
Winter's almost here, winter's almost here.
Done hung around and sung around this old town all year,
And I feel like I want to travel on.

Down By The Riverside

Traditional

1111
5555
5555
1111

Down In The Valley

Traditional

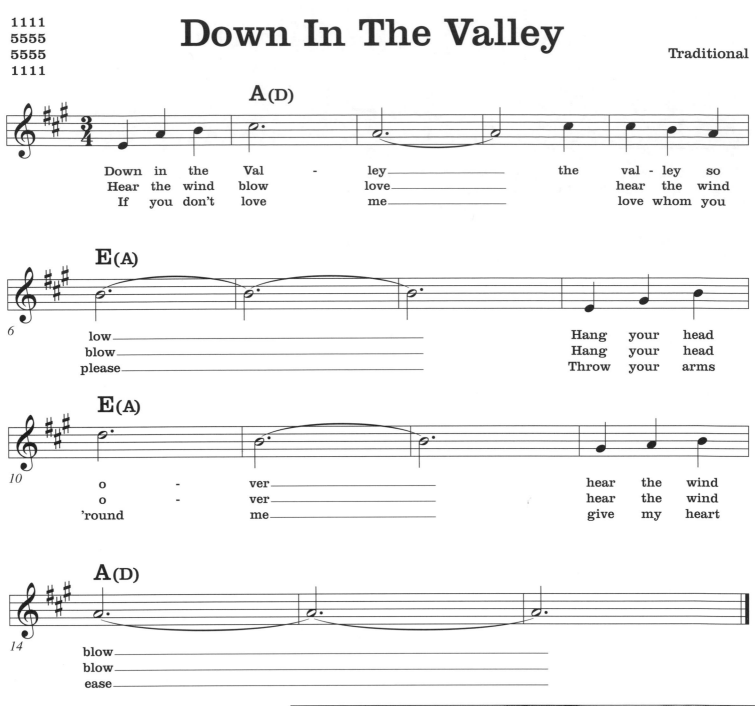

A(D)

Down in the Val - ley____ the val - ley so
Hear the wind blow love____ hear the wind
If you don't love me____ love whom you

E(A)

low____ Hang your head
blow____ Hang your head
please____ Throw your arms

E(A)

o - ver____ hear the wind
o - ver____ hear the wind
'round me____ give my heart

A(D)

blow____
blow____
ease____

Write me a letter, send it by mail
Send it in care of the Birmingham Jail

Birmingham jail love, Birmingham jail,
Send it in care of Birmingham jail

Old Town School of Folk Music

6655
6636

Drunken Sailor

Traditional

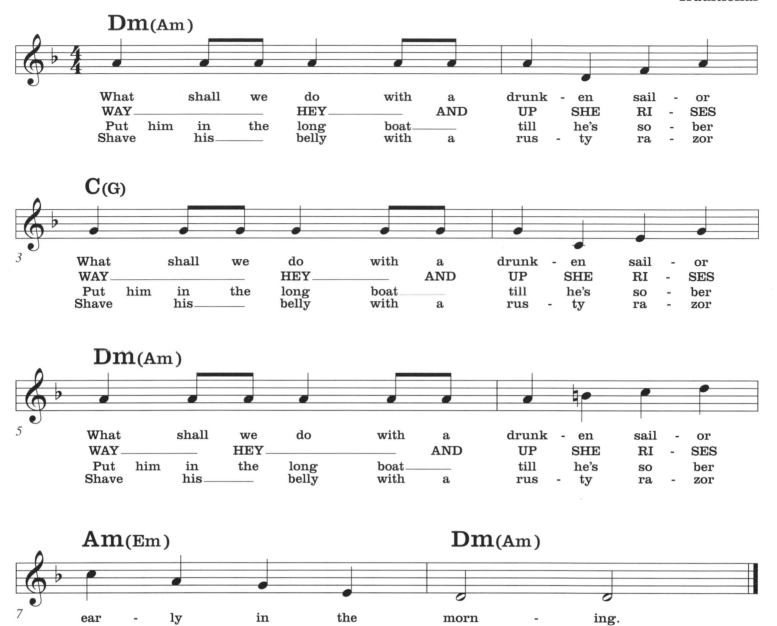

1177
5511
1144
5511

East Virginia

Traditional

I was born_____ in east Vir - gin - ia_____ North Ca-ro-
And her hair_____ was dark of co - lor_____ and her__
Ma - ma said_____ we'd ne - ver mar - ry_____ Pa - pa__

li - na I____ did__ go_____ There I
cheeks_____ were ru by red_____ On her
said_____ it'll ne - ver__ do_____ But if you

met_____ a fair young mai - den_____ whose name and
breast_____ she wore white li - lies_____ where I did
e - ver learn to love me_____ well I would

age_____ I did__ not__ know_____
long_____ to lay__ my__ head_____
run_____ a - way__ with__ you_____

Old Town School of Folk Music

El-a-noy

Traditional
as sung by Win Stracke

Erie Canal

Traditional

We were for-ty miles from Al-ba-ny, for-get it I ne-ver shall. What a
We were load-ed down with bar-ley we were chock— full up on rye, And the
The— cap-tain he came up on deck with a spy— glass in his hand And the

ter-ri-ble storm we had one night on the E-ri-e Ca-nal ⎫
cap-tain he looked down at me with-his god-damn wick-ed eye ⎬ Oh the
fog— it was so gosh darn thick that he could not spy the land ⎭

E-ri-e was a-ri-sin' and the gin was a-get-tin' low. And I

scarce-ly think we'll get a drink till we get to Buf-fa-lo-o-o till we

get to Buf-fa-lo

Two days out of Syracuse
Our vessel it struck a shoal
And we like to all been drownded
On a chunk o' Lackawanna coal
Oh the E-ri-e was risin...

Old Town School of Folk Music

Frankie & Johnny

Traditional

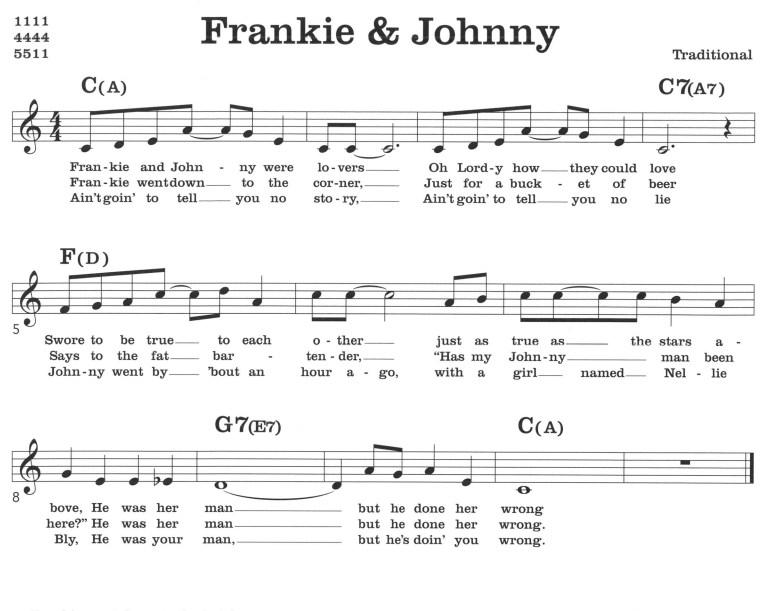

Frankie went down to the hotel
She didn't go there for fun
Underneath her kimona
She carried a forty-four gun
He was her man, but he was doin' her wrong

Frankie went down to South Clark Street
Looked in a window so high
Saw her Johnny man lovin' up
That high brow Nellie Bly
He was her man, but he done her wrong

Johnny saw Frankie a comin'
Out the back door he did scoot
But Frankie took aim with her pistol
And the gun went "Root a toot-toot!"
He was her man, but he done her wrong

Oh roll me over so easy
Roll me over so slow,
Roll me over on the right side
For the left side hurts me so
He was her man, but he was doin' her wrong

Bring on your rubber tire carriage
Bring on your rubber-tired hack
They're taking your man to the graveyard
And they ain't goin' to bring him back
He was your man, but he done you wrong.

Frankie looked out of the jailhouse
To see what she could see
All she could hear was a two-string bow
Crying, "Nearer my God to thee."
He was her man, but he was doin' her wrong

Frankie she said to the sheriff
"What do you reckon they'll do?"
Sheriff he said to Frankie,
"It's the electric chair for you."
He was her man, but he was doin' her wrong.

This story has no moral
This story has no end
This story only goes to show
That there ain't no good in men
He was her man, but he was doin' her wrong

Old Town School of Folk Music

Freight Train

Elizabeth Cotten

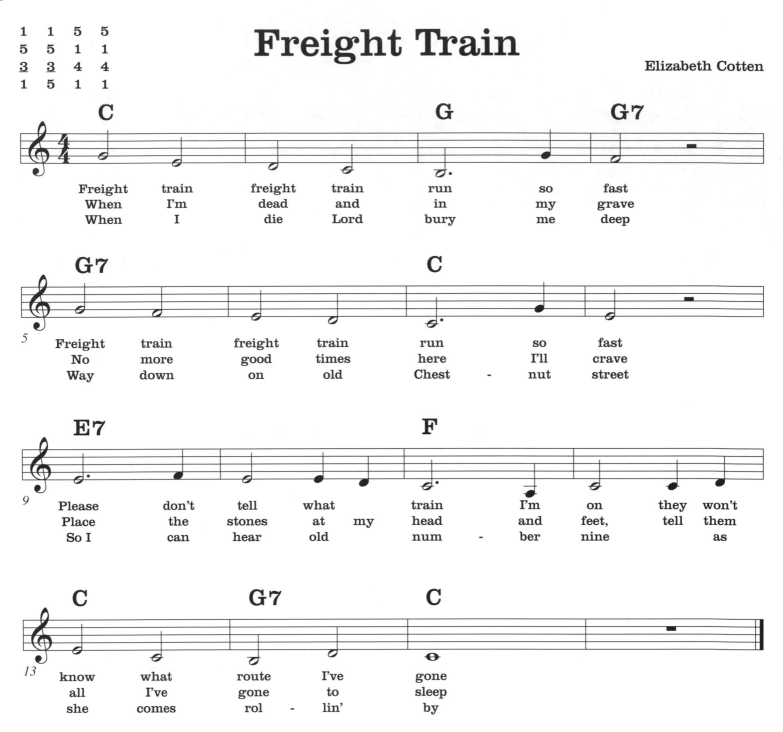

C

Freight train freight train run so fast
When I'm dead and in my grave
When I die Lord bury me deep

G7   **C**

Freight train freight train run so fast
No more good times here I'll crave
Way down on old Chest - nut street

E7   **F**

Please don't tell what train I'm on they won't
Place the stones at my head and
So I can hear old num - ber nine as

C   **G7**   **C**

know what route I've gone
all I've comes gone to sleep
she rol - lin' by

When I die Lord bury me deep
Way down on old Chestnut street
Place the stones at my head and
Feet tell them all I've gone to sleep.

Old Town School of Folk Music

Froggie Went A-Courtin'

Traditional

1 1 1 1
1 1 5 5
1 1 4 4
1 5 1 1

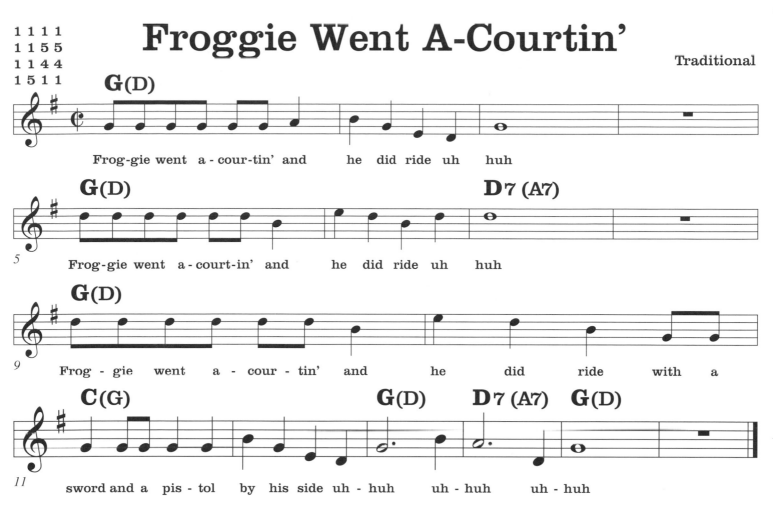

Frog-gie went a-cour-tin' and he did ride uh huh

Frog-gie went a-court-in' and he did ride uh huh

Frog - gie went a - cour - tin' and he did ride with a

sword and a pis-tol by his side uh-huh uh-huh uh-huh

Well he rode up to Miss Mousey's door, Uh-huh, (2x)
Well he rode up to Miss Mousey's door.
Gave three loud raps and a very big roar, Uh-huh.

Said, "Miss Mouse, are you within?" Uh-huh, (2x)
Said, "Miss Mouse, are you within?"
"Yes, kind sir, I sit and spin," Uh-huh.

He took Miss Mousey on his knee, Uh-huh,
Took Miss Mousey on his knee, Uh-huh,
Took Miss Mousey on his knee.
Said, "Miss Mousey, will you marry me?" Uh-huh.

"Without my uncle Rat's consent," Uh-huh (2x)
"Without my uncle Rat's consent,
I wouldn't marry the president, Uh-huh."

Uncle Rat laughed and he shook his fat sides, Uh-huh, (2x)
Uncle Rat laughed and he shook his fat sides,
To think his niece would be a bride, Uh-huh.

Uncle Rat went runnin' downtown, Uh-huh, (2x)
Uncle Rat went runnin' downtown,
To buy his niece a wedding gown, Uh-huh

Where shall the wedding supper be? Un-huh, (2x)
Where shall the wedding supper be?
Way down yonder in a hollow tree, Uh-huh

What should the wedding supper be? Uh-huh, (2x)
What should the wedding supper be?
Fried mosquito in a black-eye pea, Uh-huh.

Well, first to come in was a flyin' moth, Uh-huh,
First to come in was a flyin' moth, Uh-huh,
First to come in was a flyin' moth.
She laid out the table cloth, Uh-huh.

Next to come in was a juney bug, Uh-huh, (2x)
Next to come in was a juney bug.
She brought the water jug, Uh-huh.

Next to come in was a bumbley bee, Uh-huh (2x)
Next to come in was a bumbley bee.
Sat mosquito on his knee, Uh-huh.

Next to come in was a broken black flea, Uh-huh, (2x)
Next to come in was a broken black flea.
Danced a jig with the bumbley bee, Uh-huh.

Next to come in was Mrs. Cow, Uh-huh, (2x)
Next to come in was Mrs. Cow.
She tried to dance but she didn't know how, Uh-huh.

Next to come in was a little black tick, Uh-huh, (2x)
Next to come in was a little black tick.
She ate so much she made us sick, Uh-huh.

Next to come in was a big black snake, Uh-huh, (2x)
Next to come in was a big black snake.
Ate up all of the wedding cake, Uh-huh.

Next to come was the old gray cat, Uh-huh, (2x)
Next to come was the old gray cat.
Swallowed the mouse and ate up the rat, Uh-huh.

Mr. Frog went a-hoppin' up over the brook, Uh-huh, (2x)
Mr. Frog went a-hoppin' up over the brook.
A lily-white duck come and swallowed him up, Uh-huh.

A little piece of cornbread layin' on a shelf, Uh-huh, (2x)
A little piece of cornbread layin' on a shelf.
If you want anymore, you can sing it yourself, Uh-huh.

Git Along Little Dogies

Traditional

Goin' Down To Cairo

Traditional

Goin' 'way to leave you goodbye goodbye
Goin' 'way to leave you goodbye Liza Jane
I'll be yours if you'll be mine goodbye goodbye
I'll be yours if you'll be mine goodbye Liza Jane

Old Town School of Folk Music

Golden Slippers

James Bland

old gray horse that I used to ride I will
great camp meeting there will be that day when we
white kid gloves you will have to wear when you

hitch him to the char - iot in the morn
ride up the char - iot in the morn
ride up the char - iot in the morn

Chorus

Oh them gol - den slip-pers Oh them gol - den slip-pers

Gol - den slip-pers I'm goin' to wear be cause they look so neat

Oh them gol - den slip-pers Oh them gol - den slip-pers

Gol - den slip-pers I'm goin' to wear to walk the gol - den street

Golden Vanity

Traditional

The boy he made ready and overboard swam
He and he swam along side of the Spanish enemy
And with his brace and augur, in her side he bore holes
Three and he sunk her in the lowland lowland,
Sunk her in the lowland sea.

The boy he swam back to the cheering of the crew
But the captain would not heed him, his promise he did rue
And he cursed his poor entreaties, as loudly he did sue
And he left him in the lowland, lowland, lowland,
He left him in the lowland sea.

Old Town School of Folk Music

Good News

Traditional

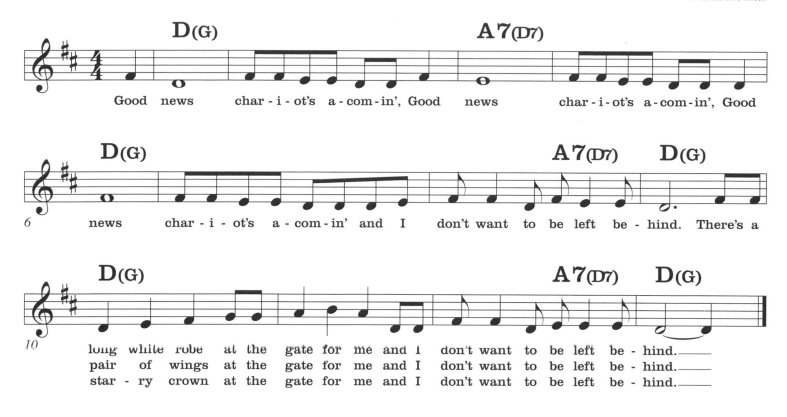

Good news char-i-ot's a-com-in', Good news char-i-ot's a-com-in', Good

news char-i-ot's a-com-in' and I don't want to be left be-hind. There's a

long white robe at the gate for me and I don't want to be left be-hind.____
pair of wings at the gate for me and I don't want to be left be-hind.____
star-ry crown at the gate for me and I don't want to be left be-hind.____

Old Town School of Folk Music

Grandfather's Clock

Henry Clay Werk

It rang an alarm in the dead of the night,
An alarm that for years had been dumb.
And we knew that his spirit was pluming its flight
That his hour of departure had come.
Still the clock kept the time with a soft and muffled chime
As we silently stood by his side,
But it stopped short never to go again
When the old man died.

Old Town School of Folk Music

Greensleeves

Traditional

Gypsy Davy

Traditional

1111
1151
51

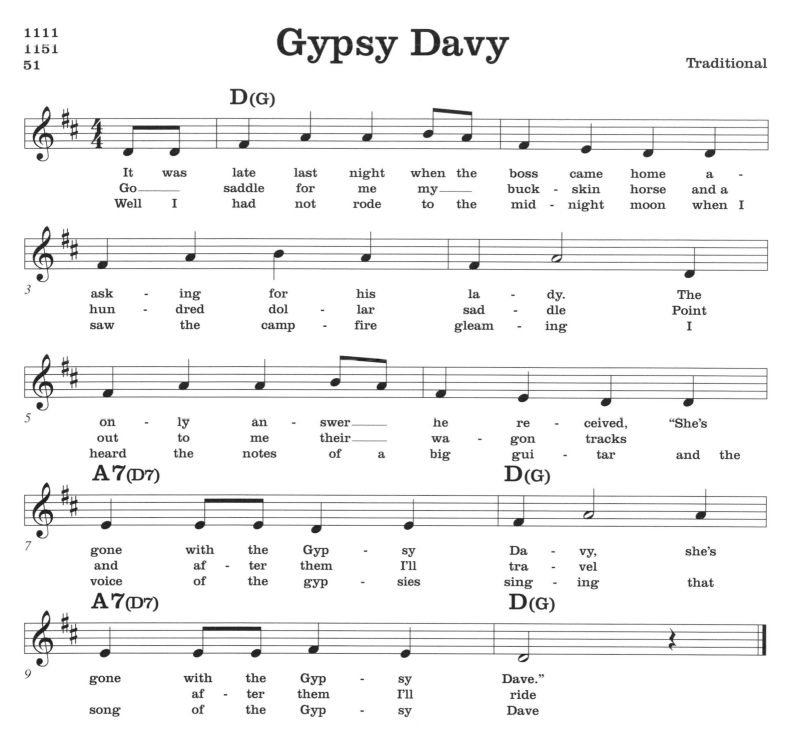

There in the light of the camping fire
I saw her fair face beaming
Her heart intune to the big guitar
And the voice of the gypsies singing
That song of Gypsy Dave

Have you forsaken your house and home
Have you foresaken your baby
Have you foresaken your husband dear
To go with the Gypsy Dave
And sing with the Gypsy Dave

Yes I've forsaken my husband dear
To go with the Gypsy Davy
And I've forsaken my mansion high
But not my blue eyed baby
Not my blue eyed babe

She smiled to leave her husband dear
And go with the Gypsy Davy
But the tears come a-trickling down her cheeks
To think of the blue eyed baby
Pretty little blue eyed babe.

Take off, take off your buckskin gloves
Made of Spanish leather
Give to me your lily-white hand
And we'll ride home together
We'll ride home again.

Now I won't take off my buckskin gloves
They're made of Spanish leather
I'll go my way from day to day
And sing with the Gypsy Davy
That song of the Gypsy Dave.

Gypsy Rover

Traditional

Hard And It's Hard

Traditional

There is a house in this town_____
First time I seen my true love_____
Don't go to drinkin' and to gamblin'_____

that's where my true love lays a - round_____ and
he was walk - in by____ my door_____ the
don't go there your sor - rows____ to drown_____ this

takes o - ther wo - men on his____ knee_____ and
last time I saw____ his_____ false - hearted smile he was
hard liquor place is a low down dis - grace_____ the

tells them things he ne - ver____ did tell me_____
dead____ on the bar - room____ floor_____ } Well it's
mean-est damn____ place____ in the town._____

hard and it's hard and its hard_____ to love one who ne - ver____ did love

you_____ well it's hard and it's hard ain't it hard great God to

love one who ne - ver____ will be true_____

1111
1155
1144
5511

Hard Travellin'

Woody Guthrie

I've been workin' that Pittsburgh steel, I thought you'd know
I been leanin' on a pressure drill from way down the road
I been blastin', I been firin'
I been duckin' red hot iron
I've been havin' some hard travelin', Lord.

Old Town School of Folk Music

Hobo's Lullaby

Reeves Gobels

1144
5511
1144
5511

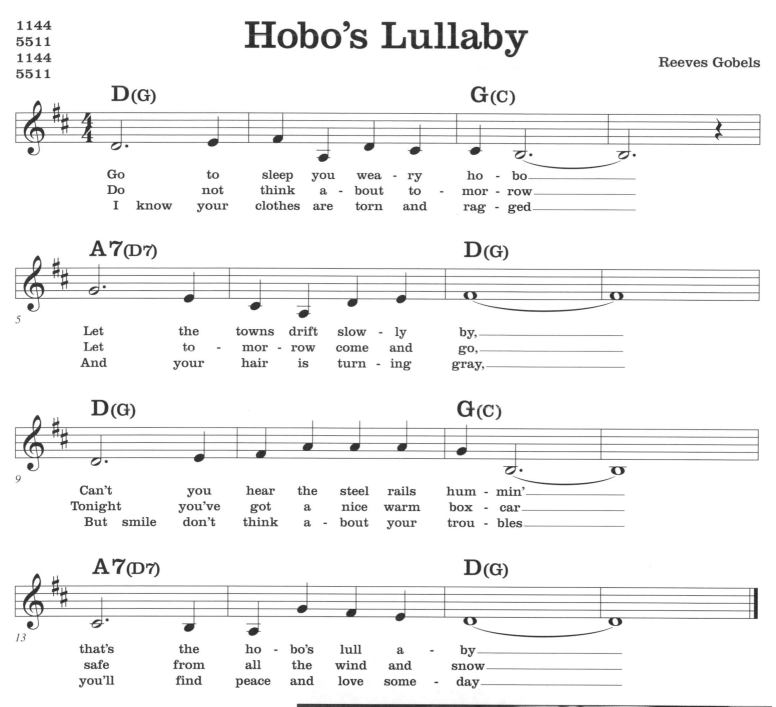

D(G)   **G**(C)

Go   to   sleep you   wea - ry   ho - bo
Do   not   think a - bout   to - mor - row
I   know your clothes are   torn   and   rag - ged

A7(D7)   **D**(G)

Let   the   towns   drift   slow - ly   by,
Let   to - mor - row come   and   go,
And   your   hair   is   turn - ing   gray,

D(G)   **G**(C)

Can't   you   hear   the   steel   rails   hum - min'
Tonight   you've got   a   nice   warm   box - car
But smile don't think a - bout   your   trou - bles

A7(D7)   **D**(G)

that's   the   ho - bo's   lull   a - by
safe   from   all   the   wind   and   snow
you'll   find   peace and   love   some - day

I know the police cause you trouble
They cause trouble every where
But when you die and go to heaven
You'll find no policemen there

Old Town School of Folk Music

Home On The Range

Traditional

G(D)   **G 7**(D7)   **C**(G)

Oh give me a home where the buf - fa - lo roam, where the
How of - ten at night when the hea - vens are bright, with the
Where the air is so pure, and the ze - phyrs so free, and the

G(D) **A 7**(E7) **D 7**(A7) **G**(D)

deer and the an - te - lope play Where sel - dom is heard a dis-
light from the glit - ter - ing stars, Have I stood there a - mazed, and
bree - zes so bal - my and light, That I would not ex - change, my

C(G) **G**(D) **D 7**(A7) **G**(D)

cou - ra - ging word, and the skies are not clou - dy all day.
asked as I gazed if their glo - ry ex - ceeds that of ours.
home on the range for all of the ci - ties so bright.

G(D) **D 7**(A7) **G**(D)   **Em**(Bm) **A 7**(E7)

Home, home on the range where the deer and the an - te - lope

D 7(A7) **G**(D) **C**(G) **Cm**(Gm)

play, where sel - dom is heard, a dis - cou - ra - ging word and the

G(D) **D 7**(A7) **G**(D)

skies are not clou - dy all day

House Of The Rising Sun

Traditional

There is a house in New Or - leans, they
My mo - ther she's a tai - lor
The on - ly thing a gam - bler needs is a

call the ri - sing sun. It's
sewed my new blue jeans My
suit - case and a trunk The

been the ru - in of ma - ny poor girls and
sweet - heart he's a gam-blin' man
on - ly time he's sa - tis - fied is

God I know I'm one
down in New Or - leans
when he's on a drunk

If I had listened to what mama said
I'd been at home today
Being so young and foolish, poor boy
Let a gambler lead me astray

Go tell my baby sister
Never do like I have done
Shun that house in New Orleans
They call the rising sun.

One foot on the platform
The other one's on the train
I'm going back to New Orleans
To wear that ball and chain

Going back to New Orleans
My race is almost run
Going back to spend my life
Beneath that rising sun.

Old Town School of Folk Music

I Am A Pilgrim

Traditional

I'm going down to the river of Jordan
Just to bathe my wearsome soul
If I can just touch the hem of His garment
Then I know He'll take me home.

World's Largest Music Lesson, August 7, 2007.

Photo by Martin Konopacki Photography

I Have No Clue

Jimmy Tomasello

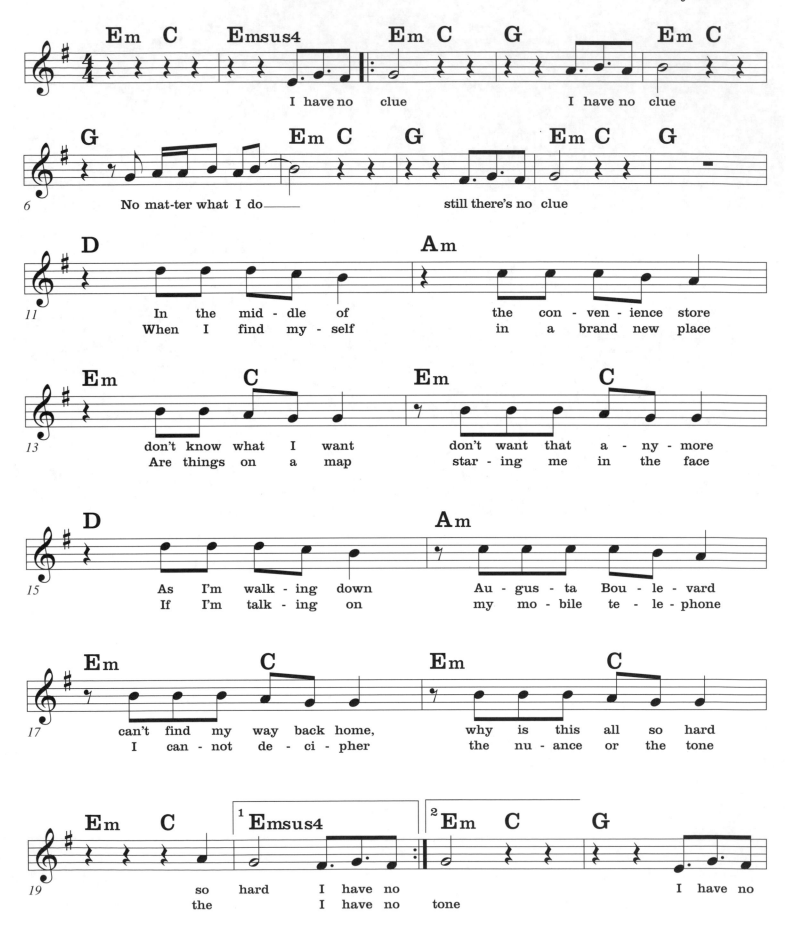

2

I Know You Rider

Traditional

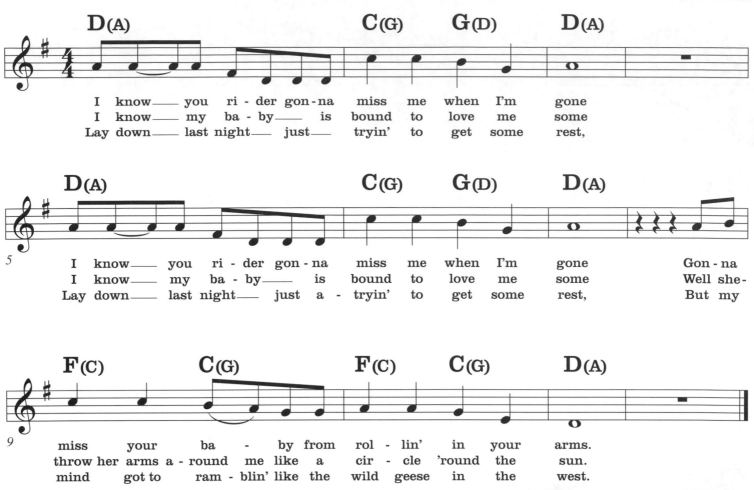

I know—— you ri - der gon-na miss me when I'm gone
I know—— my ba - by—— is bound to love me some
Lay down—— last night—— just—— tryin' to get some rest,

I know—— you ri - der gon - na miss me when I'm gone
I know—— my ba - by—— is bound to love me some
Lay down—— last night—— just a - tryin' to get some rest,

Gon - na
Well she-
But my

miss your ba - by from rol - lin' in your arms.
throw her arms a - round me like a cir - cle 'round the sun.
mind got to ram - blin' like the wild geese in the west.

Sun's gonna shine on my back door some day
Sun's gonna shine on my back door some day
And the wind's gonna blow, blow my blues away.

I wish I was a headlight, on a north bound train
I wish I was a headlight, on a north bound train
I'd shine my light through the cool Colorado rain.

Old Town School of Folk Music

I Ride An Old Paint

Traditional

1111
5511
5511
5511

I ride an old Paint— I lead an old Dan— I'm
Old Bill Jones— had a daughter and a son.— One
When I die— don't bu - ry me at all—

goin' to Mon - tan - a to throw the Hou - li - han. They
went to Den - ver and the o - ther went— wrong. His
Put me on my po - ny and lead him from his stall. Tie my

feed in the cou - lees They wa - ter in the draw their
wife she died in a pool— room— fight, but
bones to his back, turn our fa - ces to the west, and

tails are all mat - ted Their backs are all raw. Ride a -
still he keeps sing - ing from morn - in' til' night.
we'll ride the prai - ries that we love the best.

round lit - tle do - gies ride a - round— them— slow. - For the

fier - y and snuf - fy are rar - in' to go.

Old Town School of Folk Music

1155
5511
1144
1511

I'm On My Way

Traditional

G(E)

I'm on my way———— but I won't turn back I'm on my
I asked my brother———— to go with me I asked my
If he says no———— I'll go any - way If he says

D(B7)

way———— but I won't turn back———— I'm on my
brother———— to go with me———— I asked my
no———— I'll go any - way———— if he says

G(E)   G7(E7)   C(A)

way———— but I won't turn back————
brother———— to go with me———— } I'm on my
no———— I'll go any way————

G(E)   D7(B7)   G(E)

way———— great God I'm on my way————

Old Town School of Folk Music

If I Were The President

Michael J. Miles

NOTE: Make this song your own and share it with students and children by getting their presidential ideas.
Over the years Miles has surveyed thousands of Chicago public school children and sent their ideas to Washington.

Old Town School of Folk Music

In The Pines

Traditional

My love my love, don't lie to me, Tell me where did you
The long-est train I e-ver saw went___ down that___
I asked my captain the time of day, said he throwed his___

sleep last night___ In the pines in the pines where the
Geor-gia line.___ The___ en-gine passed at___
watch a way.___ A___ long steel___ rail and a

sun ne-ver shines, I would shi-ver the whole night through___
six o-clock, the___ ca-boose went by at___ nine___
short cross___ tie and___ I'll___ be on my___ way___

CHORUS
In the pines in the pines where the sun ne-ver

shines, I would shi-ver the whole night___ through___

My love my love where will you go?
Gon-na go where the cold winds blow,
Gon-na weep, gon-na cry, gon-na moan,
Gon-na sigh, gon-na dance in my good time clothes.

Jack Of Diamonds
(Cuckoo Song)

Traditional

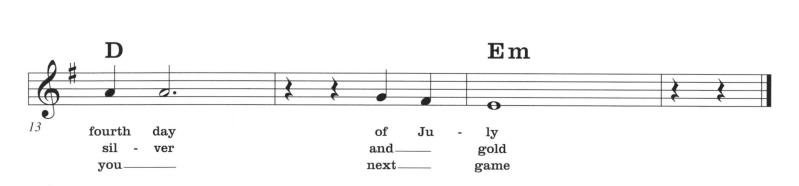

Em

Oh the Cu - ckoo_____ she's a pret-ty bird. She
Jack of Dia - monds_____ Jack of Di - a-monds I
Oh I played cards_____ in old En - gland I

D   **Em**

war - bles_____ as she flies She'll
know you_____ of_____ old You
played cards_____ in_____ Spain I'll

Em

ne - ver_____ hol - ler cu - ckoo_____ till the
rob my_____ poor_____ pock - ets_____ of their
bet you_____ ten_____ dol - lars_____ I beat

D   **Em**

fourth day of Ju - ly
sil - ver and_____ gold next_____
you_____ next_____ game

Gonna build me a log cabin
On a mountain so high
So I can see my Willy
As she goes walking by

My horses, they ain't hungry
And they won't eat your hay
I'll drive on a little further
Wondering why you treat me this way.

Old Town School of Folk Music

Jamaica Farewell

Traditional

John Barleycorn

Traditional

3. They've hired men with scythes so sharp
To cut him off at the knee
They rolled him and tied him by the waist
Serving him most barbarously
They've hired men with sharp pitch forks
Who pricked him to the heart…
And the loader he has served him worse than that
For he's bound him to the cart

4. They've wheeled him around and around in the field
'til they came onto a barn
And there they made a solemn oath
On poor John Barleycorn

(4 cont.) They've hired men with the crab tree sticks
to cut him skin from bone
And the miller he has served him worse than that
For he's ground him between two stones

5. And little Sir John and the nut brown bowl
And he's brandy in the glass
And little Sir John and the nut brown bowl
Proved the strongest man at last
The huntsman, he can't hunt the fox
Nor so loudly to blow his horn
And the Tinker he can't mend kettle nor pots
Without a little Barleycorn

Old Town School of Folk Music

John Henry

Traditional

1111
1155
1144
1144
1511

E(G)

When John Hen - ry was a lit - tle ba - by

B7(D7)

sit - tin' on his Dad - dy's knee, well he

E(G)   A7(C7)

picked up a ham - mer and a lit - tle piece of steel, said, "That

E(G)   A7(C7)

ham-mer's goin' to be the death of me, Lord,—— Lord.

E(G)   B7(D7)   E(G)

Ham-mer's goin' to be the death of me.————

The captain said to John Henry
"I'm gonna bring that steam drill around
I'm gonna bring that steam drill out on the job
I'm gonna whup that steel on down, Lord Lord
I'm gonna whup that steel on down."

John Henry told his captain
"Lord a man ain't nothin' but a man
But before I'd let your steam drill beat me down
I'd die with a hammer in my hand, Lord Lord
I'd die with a hammer in my hand."

John Henry said to his shaker,
"Shaker why don't you sing?
Because I'm swinging thirty pounds,
    from my hips on down
Just listen to that cold steel ring, Lord Lord
Listen to that cold steel ring."

Now the man that invented the steam drill
He thought he was mighty fine
But John Henry drove fifteen feet
The steam drill only made nine, Lord Lord
The steam drill only made nine.

John Henry hammered in the mountains
His hammer was striking fire
But he worked so hard, it broke his poor heart
And he laid down his hammer and he died, Lord Lord
He Laid down his hammer and he died.

So every Monday morning
When the blue birds begin to sing,
You can hear John Henry a mile or more
You can hear John Henry's hammer ring, Lord Lord
You can hear John Henry's hammer ring.

Joshua Fit The Battle Of Jericho

Traditional

Dm(Am)

Josh-ua fit the bat-tle of Je-ri-cho Je-ri-cho Je-ri-cho

Dm(Am)   **A7**(E7)   **Dm**(Am)

Josh-ua fit the bat-tle of Je-ri-cho and the walls came tum-bl-in' down You may
Way——
Then the

Dm(Am)   **A7**(E7)

talk a-bout your man of Gi-de-on You may talk a-bout your man of Saul. There's
up—— to the walls of Je-ri-cho he—— march-ed with a spear in hand. "Go
lamb, ram, and sheep horn be-gan to blow, and the trum-pets—— be-gan to sound. And

Dm(Am)   **Dm**(Am) **A7**(E7)   **Dm**(Am)

none like good old Josh-u-a at the bat-tle of Je-ri-cho.
blow the ram's horn," Josh-ua cried, "cause the bat-tle is in my hands."
Josh-ua had the chil-dren shout, and the walls—— came tumblin' down.

Old Town School of Folk Music

1 5 5 1
1 4 1-5 1

Just A Closer Walk With Thee

Traditional

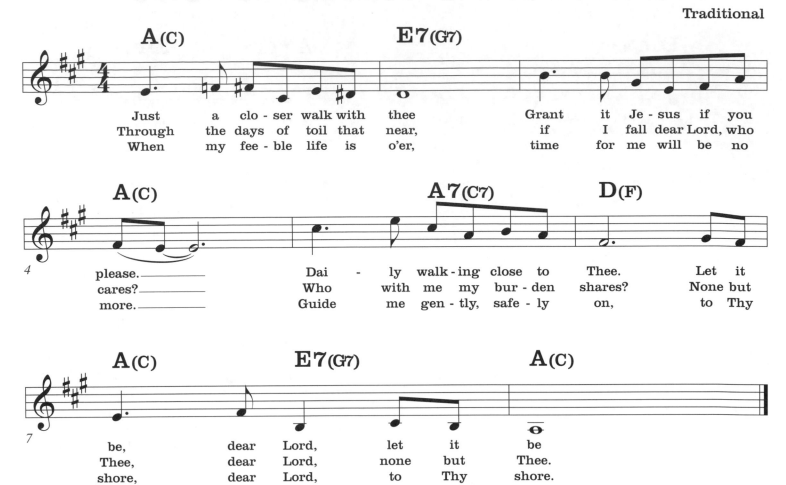

A(C)

E7(G7)

Just a clo-ser walk with thee
Through the days of toil that near,
When my fee-ble life is o'er,

Grant it Je-sus if you
if I fall dear Lord, who
time for me will be no

A(C)

A7(C7)

D(F)

please. Dai - ly walk-ing close to Thee. Let it
cares? Who with me my bur - den shares? None but
more. Guide me gen - tly, safe - ly on, to Thy

A(C)

E7(G7)

A(C)

be, dear Lord, let it be
Thee, dear Lord, none but Thee.
shore, dear Lord, to but Thy shore.

Old Town School of Folk Music

Lakes Of Ponchartrain

Traditional

'Twas on a bright March mor - nin' I bid New Or - leans a-
I stepped on board a rail - road car be - neath the mor - nin'
I said, "My pret - ty Cre - ole girl, my mo - ney here's no

dieu I took the road to Jack - son my for - tune
sun. I rode the rails 'til eve - nin' and I laid me
good. If it weren't for the al - i - ga - tors, I'd sleep out

— to re - new I cursed all fo - reign mo -
— down a - gain All strang - ers they're no friends to
— in the wood." "You're welcome here kind strang -

ney no cre - dit I could gain. I fell in love with a
me, till a dark girl to - ward me came. I fell in love with a
er our house is ve - ry plain But we ne - ver turn a—

Cre - ole girl by the Lakes of Ponch - ar - train.
Cre - ole girl by the Lakes of Ponch - ar - train.
strang - er out on the Lakes of Ponch - ar - train.

She took me to her Mama's house
and treated me right well
The hair upon her shoulders
in jet black ringlets fell
To try and paint her beauty
I'm sure would be in vain
So handsome was my Creole girl
by the Lakes of Ponchartrain

I asked her would she marry me
She said that would never be
For she had a lover
and he was far at sea
She promised to wait for him
And true she would remain
'til he returned to his Creole girl
on the Lakes of Ponchartrain

So fare thee well my Creole girl
I'll never see you no more
I'll never forget your kindness
in the cottage bythe shore
And at every social gathering
a golden glass I'll drain
And drink all health to my Creole
girl on the Lakes of Ponchartrain

Old Town School of Folk Music

Last Thing On My Mind

Tom Paxton

It's a les-son — too late for the learn-ing — made of sand,
made of sand. In the wink of an eye my soul is turn-ing —
in your hand, in your hand.

Chorus

Are you go - ing a - way with no word of fare - well? Will there be not a trace left be - hind? Well I could have loved you bet-ter di-dn't mean to be un kind. — You know that was the last — thing on my mind. —

As we walk all my thoughts are a tumblin'
'Round and 'round, 'round and 'round
Underneath our feet, the subway's rumblin'
Underground, underground.

You have reasons a-plenty for goin'
this I know, this I know.
For the weeds have been steadily growin'
Please don't go, please don't go.

As I lie in my bed in the morning
Without you, without you
Each song in my breast dies a-borning,
Without you, without you.

1111
4411
4411
5511

Lonesome Road Blues
(Goin' Down The Road)

Traditional

E(G)

I'm goin' down the road feel-in' bad,_____ I'm
I'm goin' where the climate suits my clothes,_____ I'm
I'm goin' where the climate chilly wind don't blow,_____ I'm

A(C)   E(G)

goin' down the road feel-in bad,_____ I'm
goin' where the climate suits my clothes,_____ I'm
goin' where the chilly wind don't blow,_____ I'm

A(C)   E(G)

goin' down the road feel-in' bad, Lord, Lord___ I
goin' where the climate suits my clothes, Lord, Lord___ I
goin' where the chilly winds don't blow, Lord, Lord___ I

B7(D7)   E(G)

ain't gon - na be treat-ed this a way._____
ain't gon - na be treat-ed this a way._____
ain't gon - na be treat-ed this a way._____

Those two dollar shoes hurt my feet
These two dollar shoes hurt my feet
These two dollar shoes hurt my feet, Lord Lord
These ten dollar shoes feel just fine

Old Town School of Folk Music

Make Me Down A Pallet

Traditional

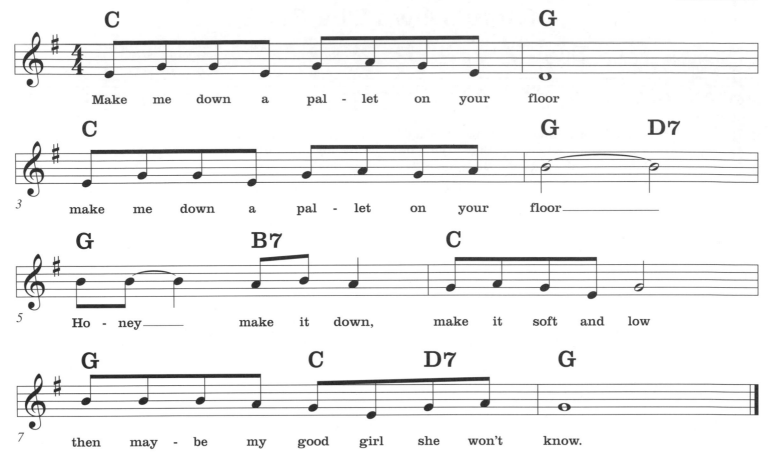

Make me down a pal - let on your floor

make me down a pal - let on your floor____

Ho - ney____ make it down, make it soft and low

then may - be my good girl she won't know.

Up the country, where there's sleet and snow
Up the country where there's sleet and snow,
I'm goin' up the country where there's sleet and snow,
No tellin' how much further I may go.

Way I've been sleepin', my back and shoulders' tired,
Way I've been sleepin', my back and shoulders' tired
This way I've been sleepin', my back and shoulders' tired
Goin' turn over and try it on the side.

Don't you let my good girl catch you here
Please don't let my good girl catch you here
Or she might shoot you, might cut and stab you, too,
Ain't no tellin' just what she might do.

Worried blues are everywhere I see
These worried blues are everywhere I see
These blues are all around me, they're everywhere I go
Make me down a pallet on your floor.

Old Town School of Folk Music

4411
5511

Midnight Special

Traditional

Well you wake up in the mor-ning, hear the ding dong ring, You go mar-ching to the
If you e - ver been to Hous-ton, you bet - ter walk right, You bet - ter not
Yon-der comes Miss Ro - sy; How in the world did you know? I know her by her

ta - ble, see the same damn thing: Well, it's all on the
stag - ger, you bet - ter not fight. Sher - iff Ben-son will ar-
ap - ron, and the dress she wore. Um - brel - la on her

ta - ble, knife, a fork and a pan, And if you say a thing a-
rest you, and the boys will bring you down, And you can bet your bot - tom
shoul - der, piece of pap-er in her hand, She goes a-march-ing to the

bout it, you're in trou - ble with the man. Let the mid - night
dol - lar, you're Sugar - land bound.
cap - tain, says I want my man.

spe - cial, shine her light on me; Let the mid - night

spe - cial shine her e - ver lo - vin' light on me

NOTE: Chorus is often played as written with only seven measures, not eight.

Old Town School of Folk Music

My Home's Across The Smoky Mountains

1111
5511

Traditional

D(A)

My   home's   a - cross the   Smo - ky   Moun   -   tains.   My
Good   - bye   ho - ney   su - gar dar   -   lin'_____
Rock   my   ba - by   give   her   can   -   day_____
Where's   that   fin - ger ring   I   gave   you_____

A7(E7)   **D(A)**

home's   a - cross the   Smo - ky   Moun   -   tains.   My
Good   - bye   ho - ney   su - gar dar_____   lin'
Rock   my   ba - by   give   her   can   -   dy,   Go
Where's   that   fin - ger ring   I   gave_____   you.   Now

D(A)

home's   a   cross   the   Smo - ky   Moun   -   tains,   and   I'll
Good   - bye   ho - ney   su - gar dar   -   lin'
rock   my   ba - by   give   her   can   -   dy
where's   that   fin - ger ring   I   gave   you?

A7(E7)   **D(A)**

ne - ver get   to   see   you   a - ny   more,   more   more.   I'll

A7(E7)   **D(A)**

ne - ver get   to   see   you   a - ny   more_____

Old Town School of Folk Music

New River Train

Traditional

Darlin' you can't love three
You can't love three and be true to me.

Darlin' you can't love four
You can't love four and walk through the door.

Darlin' you can't love five
You can't love five and hope to stay alive.

Old Town School of Folk Music

Nine Hundred Miles

Traditional

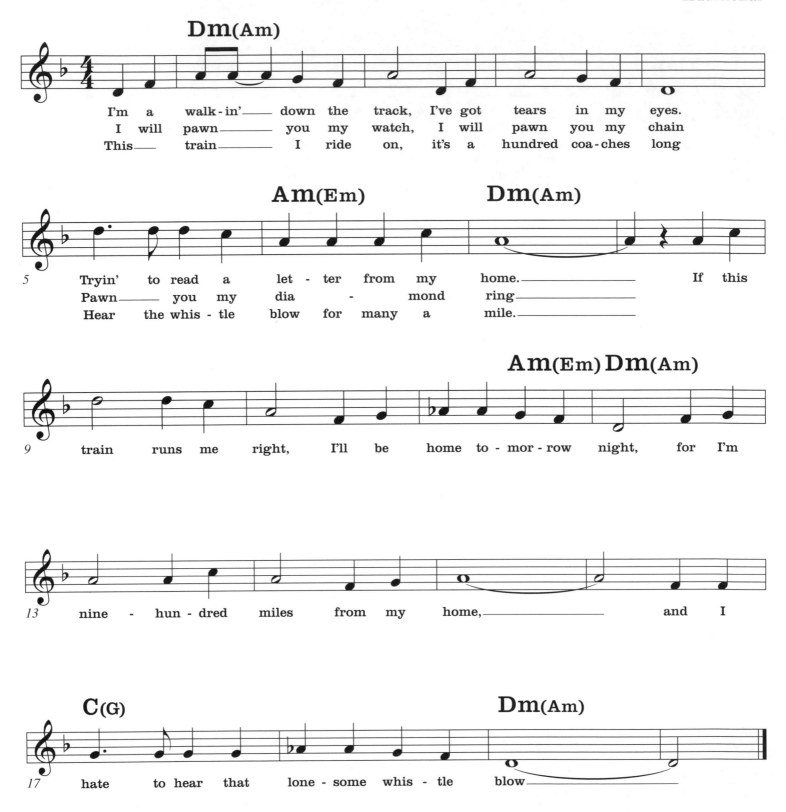

Oh Mary Don't You Weep

Traditional

God gave Noah the Rainbow sign
No more water but fire next time
Pharoah's army got drownded...

Oh Susanah

Stephen Foster

Old Blue

Traditional

I had an old dog and his name was Blue, I
I took my axe and I took my horn I
Well pos - sum crawled out on a limb. Blue
When I get to heaven first thing I'll do, when

had an old dog and his name was Blue, I
went to find a possum in the new round corn. Then
barked at possum, pos - sum new growled at him. Well
I get to heaven first thing I'll do When

had an old dog and his name was Blue
Old Blue treed and I went to see
he treed possum in a hol - low log.
I get to heaven first thing I'll do,

Bet ya five dol - lars he's a good dog too
Blue had a pos - sum up in a tree
You could tell he was a good old dog
Get out my horn and call Old Blue

Chorus:

Here Blue you're a good dog, you

Old Town School of Folk Music

Old Dog Tray

Stephen Foster

1155
1451

Old Time Religion

Traditional

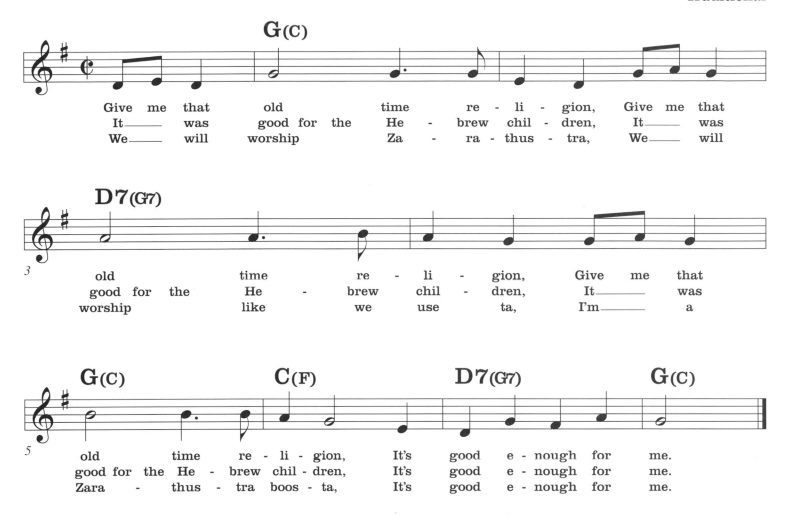

G(C)

Give me that old time re - li - gion, Give me that
It___ was good for the He - brew chil - dren, It___ was
We___ will worship Za - ra - thus - tra, We___ will

D7(G7)

old time re - li - gion, Give me that
good for the He - brew chil - dren, It___ was
worship like we use ta, I'm___ a

G(C)   C(F)   D7(G7)   G(C)

old time re - li - gion, It's good e - nough for me.
good for the He - brew chil - dren, It's good e - nough for me.
Zara - thus - tra boos - ta, It's good e - nough for me.

We will worship like the Druids
Drinking strange fermented fluids
Running naked through the wuids
And it's good enough for me

We will workship good ol' Buddha
Among the gods there is none cuter
Comes in silver, brass, or pewter
And it's good enough for me.

Old Town School of Folk Music

Old Town Old Friend

Chris Farrell

1115
5551

Pay Me My Money Down

Traditional

I thought I heard the cap - tain say pay me my mon-ey down, to-
The very next day we cleared the bar, pay me my mon-ey down, he
I wish I was Mister How - ward's son pay me my mon-ey down, sit

mor - row is my sail - ing day,___ pay me my mon-ey down.___
knocked me down with the end of a spar,___ pay me my mon-ey down.___
in the house and drink good rum,___ pay me my mon-ey down.___

Pay me, oh pay me, pay me my mon - ey down.___

Pay me or go to jail.___ Pay me my mon - ey down.___

Old Town School of Folk Music

1115
5551

Polly Wolly Doodle

Traditional

Oh I went to bed but it was no use
My feet stuck out like a chicken roost

Behind the barn down on my knees
I thought I heard a chicken sneeze

He sneezed so hard with a whooping cough
He sneezed his head and tail right off.

Old Town School of Folk Music

Ramblin' Boy

Tom Paxton

He was a man—— and a friend al - ways He stuck with me——
To Tul - sa town,—— we—— chanced to stray. We thought we'd try
Was late one night—— in the jun - gle camp, the wea - ther it——
My ram-blin' pal—— he's dead and gone. He left me here——

—— in the hard old days. He ne - ver cared if I had no
—— for—— work one day. The boss said he had—— work for
—— was—— cold and damp. He got the chills, and he got 'em
—— to—— ram - ble on. If when we die we—— go some-

dough We ram - bled a - round in the rain and snow
one. Said—— my—— old pal, we'd ra - ther bum
bad. I—— lost—— the on - ly—— friend I had
where I bet you—— a dollar he's—— ram-blin' there

And here's to you my ram-blin' boy, may all your

ram - bles bring you joy. And here's to you my ram - blin'

boy may all you ram - blin' bring you joy——

Old Town School of Folk Music

1511
1155
1144
5511

Red River Valley

Traditional

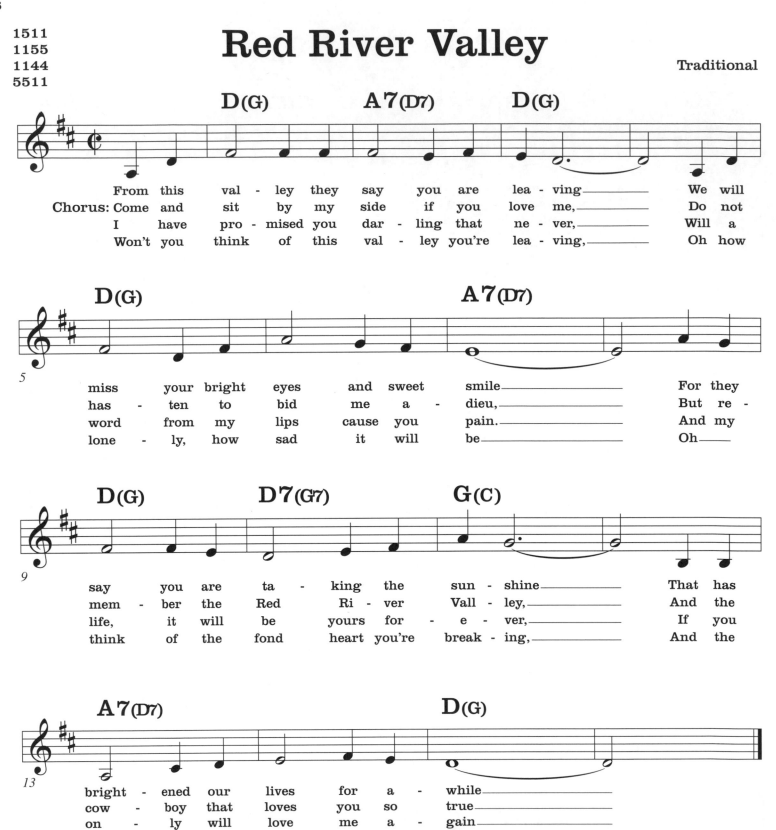

Rivers of Babylon

Traditional

Rodrigo's Gold

Eric Lugosch
Jim DeWan

Rod - ri-go was— a sai - lor and he sailed the se - ven seas—— first mate to Co-lum-

bus in the fif-teenth cen - tu - ry——— He bought the whole— sto - ry how the

world was round— Let faith fill— the sails boys andwe'll-sure-ly hit—some ground—

Six weeks in the men got strick-en with fear, Could-n't— help— but

think that the edge was near——

it's a long way down a long way down

Columbus pulled the reins in and gave his command
With the promise of gold to the first to spot the land
Rodrigo watched and prayed for what no man had seen
With gold in his eyes, he found that patch of green

Rodrigo bowed his head and prayed for his reward
Columbus took that sack of gold and dropped it
overboard. Its a long way down

A man can earn his pay and never ask for more
Six weeks till his pension and they show him the door
No way to make the mortgage so they take the land away
Sixty-four and homeless, no way to end your days

When the preacher says, "We all get our reward"
All I know is what I know for sure
It's a long way down

Things haven't changed much since Rodrigo's day
We got the rug beneath our feet, and then it's pulled away
It's a long way down.

Old Town School of Folk Music

Roll In My Sweet Baby's Arms

Traditional

1111
1155
1144
5511

I ain't gon - na work on —— the rail - road | I
Now some - times there's a change in —— the o - cean | And
My ma - ma's —— a gin - ger —— cake ba - ker | My
Now where were —— you last —— Fri - day night | While

ain't gon - na work on —— the farm | Lay 'round the shack till the
some - times a change in —— the sea | Some - times a change in my
sis - ter —— can weave and —— spin | Dad - dy's got interest in that
I —— was locked up —— in jail? | Walk - in the streets with a -

mail - train comes back, just roll in my sweet ba - by's arms.
own true l love but ne - ver a change in —— me
old cot - ton mill, just watch all the mo - ney roll in
no - ther —— man. You couldn't e - ven go my —— bail

Roll in my sweet ba - by's arms Roll in my sweet ba - by's arms Lay 'round the

shack till the mail - train comes back, just roll in my sweet ba - by's arms

Old Town School of Folk Music

1155
b7411

Roll Me On The Water

Bonnie Koloc

There are few blue-eyed men I would choose to be - lieve in this
There are few fair-haired men I would choose to be - lieve in this
And if I were in the forest with the darkness all a - round I'd sleep ba - by

wide world a - round. But if I were on the o - cean with the
wide world a - round. But if I were fall - ing from the
there in your arms But when I would a - wa - ken I would

waves all a - round me, I'd lean ba - by right back in your arms Ba - by
high - est moun - tain, I'd lean ba - by right back in your arms.
look in - to your eyes and know that I had been found

roll me on the wa - ter, roll me on the wa - ter take me

right down to the shore Roll me on the wa - ter,

roll me on the wa - ter Take me right down on the floor

Old Town School of Folk Music

Salty Dog Blues

Traditional

Scarborough Fair

Traditional

Tell her to find me an acre of land
Parsley sage rosemary and thyme
Between the saltwater and the sea strand
Then she'll be a true love of mine.

Old Town School of Folk Music

Set All God's Children Free

Bruce Roper

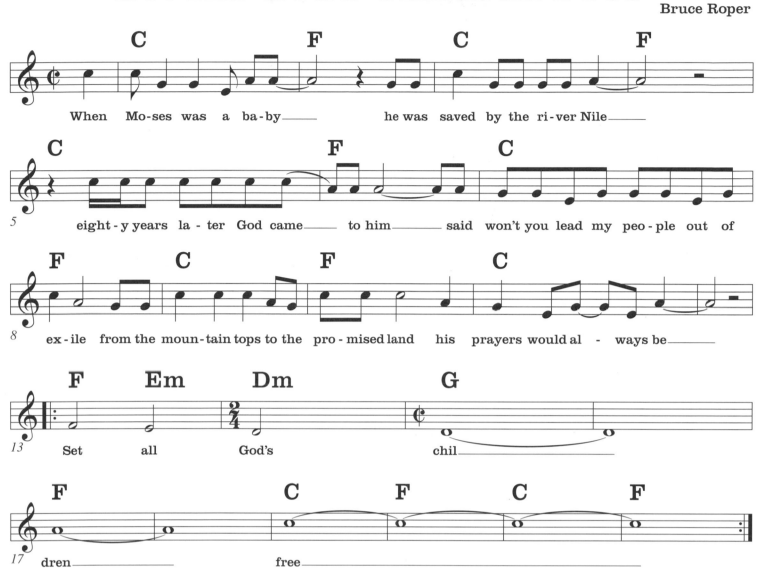

When Mo-ses was a ba-by—— he was saved by the ri-ver Nile——

eight-y years la-ter God came—— to him—— said won't you lead my peo-ple out of

ex-ile from the moun-tain tops to the pro-mised land his prayers would al - ways be——

Set all God's chil—— dren—— free——

And when Lincoln came to Illinois, he communed at the mighty Mississip'
And as he drank he realized the River Jordan at his lips
The River rose up and it begged on him, "when these waters reach the sea"
Set all God's children free, set all God's children free.

When Crazy Horse was parted by the white man from this earth
His spirit rose, Sioux legend goes, and it cried out at this birth
"Won't you bury my heart beside the waters of the creek called Wounded Knee"
And set all God's children free, set all God's children free.

Listen, listen to the waters of today, it's a million tears that make the river run
Compassion makes it stay, and it will sing to you
A thousand songs of thought and word and deed
Set all God's children free, set all God's children free.

Old Town School of Folk Music

6566
6556

Shady Grove

Traditional

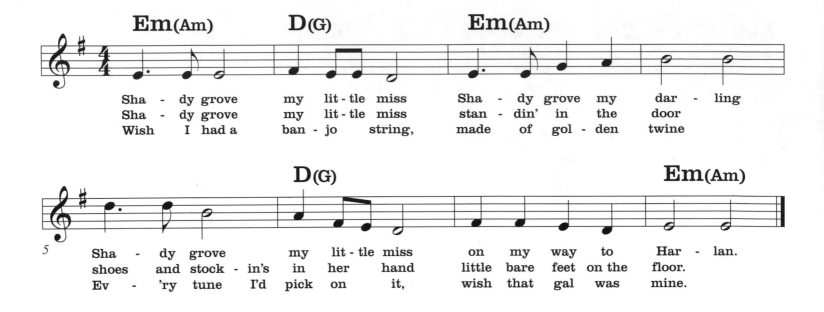

Sha - dy grove   my lit - tle miss   Sha - dy grove my   dar - ling
Sha - dy grove   my lit - tle miss   stan - din' in the   door
Wish I had a   ban - jo string,   made of gol - den   twine

Sha - dy grove   my lit - tle miss   on my way to   Har - lan.
shoes and stock - in's in her hand   little bare feet on the   floor.
Ev - 'ry tune I'd pick on it,   wish that gal was   mine.

Peaches in the summertime, apples in the fall
If I can't get the girl I love, I won't have none at all

Coffee grows on a white oak tree, river flows with brandy
I'm in love with a pretty little miss, sweet as sugar candy.

Shenandoah

Traditional

Oh Shenandoah I love your daughter
Away, you rolling river-
For her I'd crossed the rolling water,
Away we're bound away,
'Cross the wide Missouri.

Shine On Harvest Moon

Jack and Nora Norworth

Old Town School of Folk Music

Simple Gifts

Traditional

'Tis a gift to be loving, 'tis the best give of all,
Like a warm, spring rain bringing beauty when it falls,
And when we use this gift we may come to believe
It is better to give than it is to receive.

Old Town School of Folk Music

Skip To My Lou

Traditional

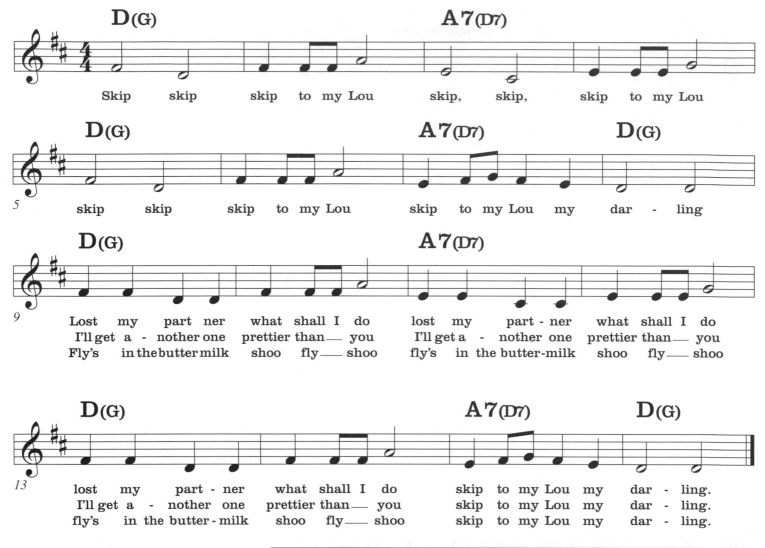

Skip skip skip to my Lou skip, skip, skip to my Lou

skip skip skip to my Lou skip to my Lou my dar - ling

Lost my part ner what shall I do lost my part - ner what shall I do
I'll get a - nother one prettier than— you I'll get a - nother one prettier than— you
Fly's in the butter milk shoo fly— shoo fly's in the butter-milk shoo fly— shoo

lost my part - ner what shall I do skip to my Lou my dar - ling.
I'll get a - nother one prettier than— you skip to my Lou my dar - ling.
fly's in the butter - milk shoo fly— shoo skip to my Lou my dar - ling.

Little red wagon painted blue
Little red wagon painted blue
Little red wagon painted blue
Skip to my Lou my darling.

Old Town School of Folk Music

Sloop John B

Traditional

Sportin' Life Blues

Traditional

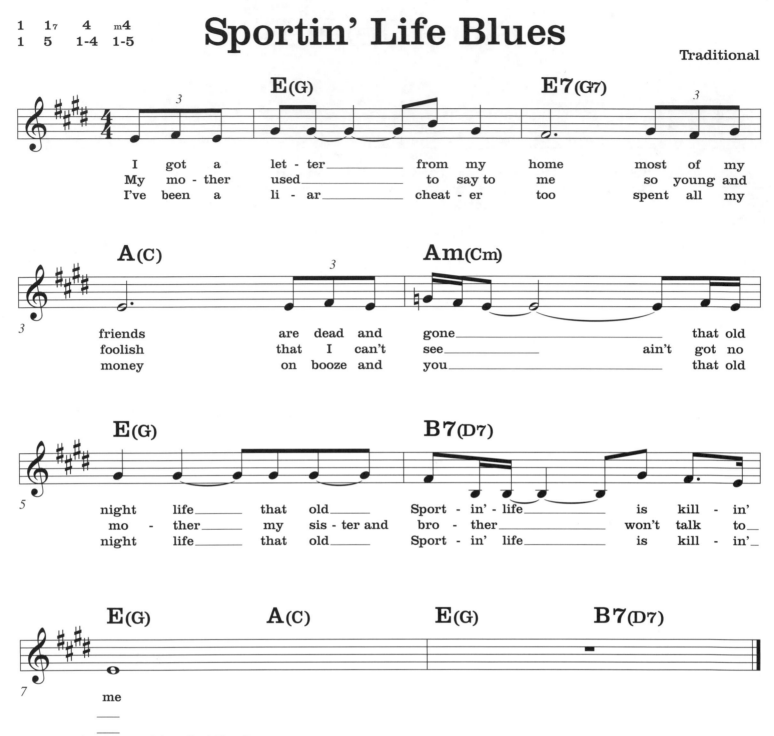

There ain't but one thing that I've done wrong
Lived this sportin' life, my friend, too long
I say it's no good, please believe me,
Please leave it alone

St. James Infirmary

Traditional

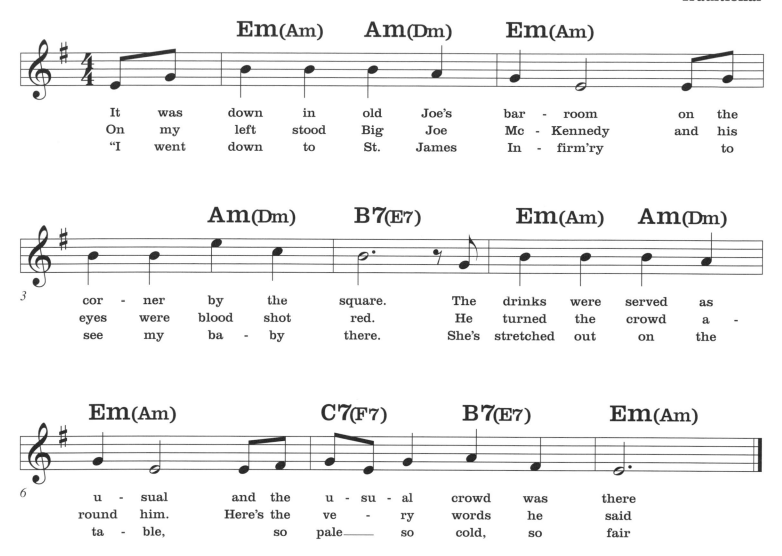

It was down in old Joe's bar-room on the
On my left stood old Big Joe Mc-Kennedy and his
"I went down to St. James In-firm'ry to

cor-ner by the square. The drinks were served as
eyes were blood shot red. He turned the crowd a-
see my ba-by there. She's stretched out on the

u-sual and the u-su-al crowd was there
round him. Here's the ve-ry words he said
ta-ble, so pale so cold, so fair

Let her go, let her go, God bless her
Wherever she may be
She may search this whole world over
Never find a man as sweet as me

When I die, please bury me
In a high-top Stetson hat.
Put a 20 dollar gold piece on my watch chain
The gang'll know I died standing pat

I want six crap shooters for pall bearers
Six pretty gals to sing me a song
Put a jazz band on my hearse wagon
To raise hell as we stroll along

And now that you've heard my story
I'll have another shot of booze
And if anybody happens to ask you
I've got the St. James Infirmary blues

Old Town School of Folk Music

Stealin'

Traditional

The woman that I'm lovin'
She's just my height and size
She's a married woman
Come to see me somtime.
If you don't believe I love you
Look what I fool I've benn
If you don't believe I'm sinkin'
Look at the hole I'm in.

Stewball

1166
2222
5555
1411

Traditional

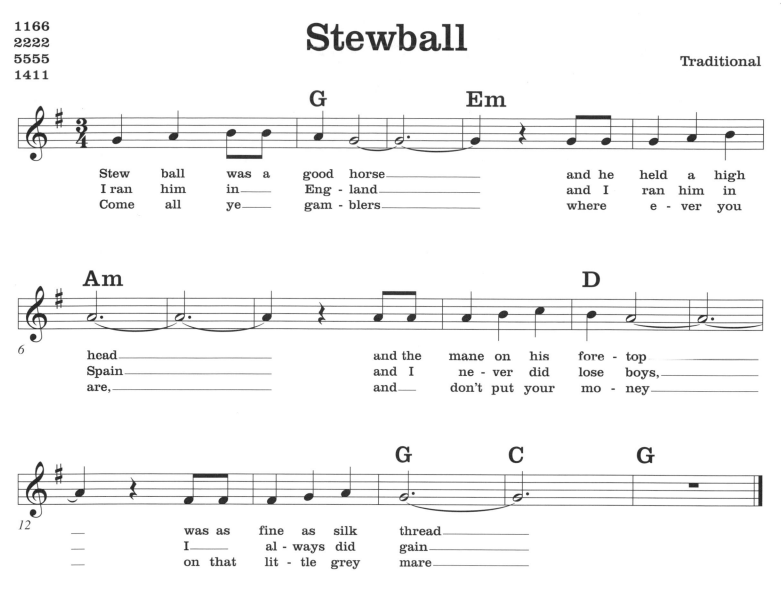

Stew ball was a good horse and he held a high
I ran him in Eng - land and I ran him in
Come all ye gam - blers where e - ver you

head and the mane on his fore - top
Spain and I ne - ver did lose boys,
are, and don't put your mo - ney

was as fine as silk thread
I al - ways did gain
on that lit - tle grey mare

Most likely she'll stumble
Most likely she'll fall
But you never will lose boys
On your noble Stewball

Sit tight in your saddle
Let slack on your rein
And you never will lose boys
You always will gain

And as they were riding
'Bout half the way round
That gray mare she stumbled
And fell to the ground

And way out yonder
Ahead of them all
Came prancing and dancing
My noble stewball

Old Town School of Folk Music

Swing Low Sweet Chariot

Traditional

Swing low sweet cha - ri - ot____ com-in' for to car-ry me home Swing____

low sweet cha - ri - ot____ com-in' for to car-ry me home. I
If

looked o - ver Jor - dan and what did I see____ com-in' for to car-ry me home a
you get____ there____ be - fore____ I do____ com-in' for to car-ry me home tell

band of an - gels com-in' af - ter me____ com-in' for to car-ry me home.
all my friends____ I'm com-in' home____ too____ com-in' for to car-ry me home.

Old Town School of Folk Music

Take This Hammer

Traditional

I don't want no cold iron shackles
I don't want no cold iron shackles
I don't want no cold iron shackles
Around my leg, around my leg

Tell Old Bill

Traditional

They brought Bill home in a hurry up wagon this morning
They brought Bill home in a hurry up wagon this evening
They brought Bill home in a hurry up wagon
Poor dead Bill his toes were draggin'
This morning, this evening, so soon.

Old Town School of Folk Music

This Train

Traditional

1111
1155
1144
1511

This train is bound for glory this train
This train don't carry no gam-blers this train
This train done carried my mo-ther this train

This train is bound for glory this train
This train don't carry no gam-blers this train
This train done carried my mo-ther this train

This train is bound for glo-ry don't ride no-thin' but the right-eous and the ho-ly,
This train don't carry no gam-blers no crap shoot-ers no mid-night ram-blers,
This train done carried my mother my father my mo-ther my sis-ter my bro-ther,

This train is bound for glo-ry this train.
This train don't carry no gam-blers this train.
This train done carried my mo-ther this train.

This train don't pay no transportation this train *(Repeat 3 times)*
No Jim Crow, no discrimination
This train don't pay no transportation this train

This train don't carry no rustlers, this train *(Repeat 3 times)*
No side street walkers, no two-bit hustlers
This train don't carry no rustlers, this train

Old Town School of Folk Music

The Walrus And The Carpenter

Words: Lewis Carroll
Music: Steve Levitt

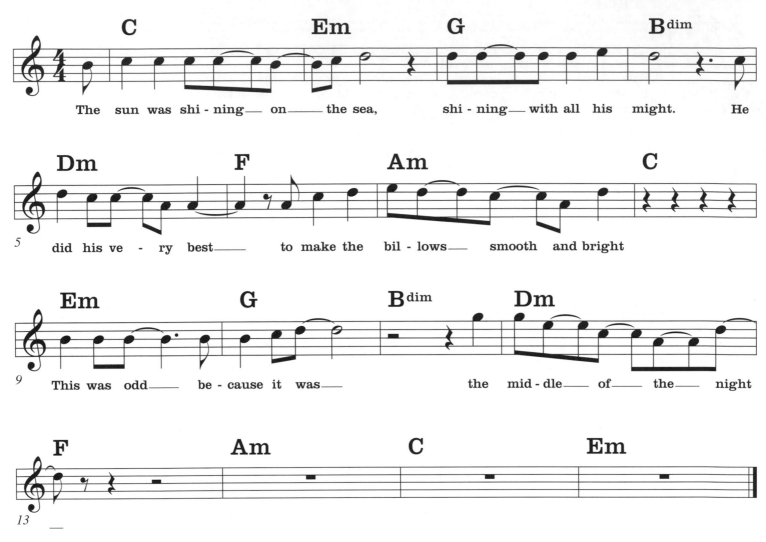

The sun was shi-ning— on— the sea, shi-ning— with all his might. He

did his ve - ry best— to make the bil-lows— smooth and bright

This was odd— be - cause it was— the mid-dle— of— the— night

NOTE: The music works like geometric magic. The 16 measure chord progression repeats over and over throughout the song. The vocal part of each verse starts two measures further into the progression with each verse.

IE. Verse 1 starts on measure 1 (C); verse 2 starts on measure 3(G); verse 3 starts on measure 5 (Dm). The starting chord is given for each verse.

G
The moon was shining sulkily,
 Because she thought the sun
 Had got no business to be there
 After the day was done--
 "It's very rude of him," she said,
 "To come and spoil the fun!"

Dm
 The sea was wet as wet could be,
 The sands were dry as dry.
 You could not see a cloud, because
 No cloud was in the sky:
 No birds were flying overhead--
 There were no birds to fly.

Am
 The Walrus and the Carpenter
 Were walking close at hand;
 They wept like anything to see
 Such quantities of sand:
 "If this were only cleared away,"
 They said, "it would be grand!"

Em
 "If seven maids with seven mops
 Swept it for half a year.
 Do you suppose," the Walrus said,
 "That they could get it clear?"
 "I doubt it," said the Carpenter,
 And shed a bitter tear.

Bdim
 "O Oysters, come and walk with us!"
 The Walrus did beseech.
 "A pleasant walk, a pleasant talk,
 Along the briny beach:
 We cannot do with more than four,
 To give a hand to each."

C
The eldest Oyster looked at him,
 But never a word he said:
 The eldest Oyster winked his eye,
 And shook his heavy head--
 Meaning to say he did not choose
 To leave the oyster-bed.

G
But four young Oysters hurried up,
 All eager for the treat:
 Their coats were brushed, their faces washed,
 Their shoes were clean and neat--
 And this was odd, because, you know,
 They hadn't any feet.

Dm
Four other Oysters followed them,
 And yet another four;
 And thick and fast they came at last,
 And more, and more, and more--
 All hopping through the frothy waves,
 And scrambling to the shore.

Am
 The Walrus and the Carpenter
 Walked on a mile or so,
 And then they rested on a rock
 Conveniently low:
 And all the little Oysters stood
 And waited in a row.

Em
 "The time has come," the Walrus said,
 "To talk of many things:
 Of shoes--and ships--and sealing-wax--
 Of cabbages--and kings--
 And why the sea is boiling hot--
 And whether pigs have wings."

Bdim
 "But wait a bit," the Oysters cried,
 "Before we have our chat;
 For some of us are out of breath,
 And all of us are fat!"
 "No hurry!" said the Carpenter.
 They thanked him much for that.

C
 "A loaf of bread," the Walrus said,
 "Is what we chiefly need:
 Pepper and vinegar besides
 Are very good indeed--
 Now if you're ready, Oysters dear,
 We can begin to feed."

Old Town School of Folk Music

Interlude:
F Am C Em G Bdim Dm F
Am C Em G   Bdim Dm F Am

G
"But not on us!" the Oysters cried,
 Turning a little blue.
 "After such kindness, that would be
 A dismal thing to do!"
 "The night is fine," the Walrus said.
 "Do you admire the view?

Dm
 "It was so kind of you to come!
 And you are very nice!"
 The Carpenter said nothing but
 "Cut us another slice:
 I wish you were not quite so deaf--
 I've had to ask you twice!"

Am
 "It seems a shame," the Walrus said,
 "To play them such a trick,
 After we've brought them out so far,
 And made them trot so quick!"
 The Carpenter said nothing but
 "The butter's spread too thick!"

Em
 "I weep for you," the Walrus said:
 "I deeply sympathize."
 With sobs and tears he sorted out
 Those of the largest size,
 Holding his pocket-handkerchief
 Before his streaming eyes.

Bdim
 "O Oysters," said the Carpenter,
 "You've had a pleasant run!
 Shall we be trotting home again?'
 But answer came there none--
 And this was scarcely odd, because
 They'd eaten every one.

Outro:
F Am C Em
G Bdim Dm F
Am C Em G
Bdim Dm F Am C

Old Town School of Folk Music

The Water Is Wide

Traditional

1411
6625
3464
1411

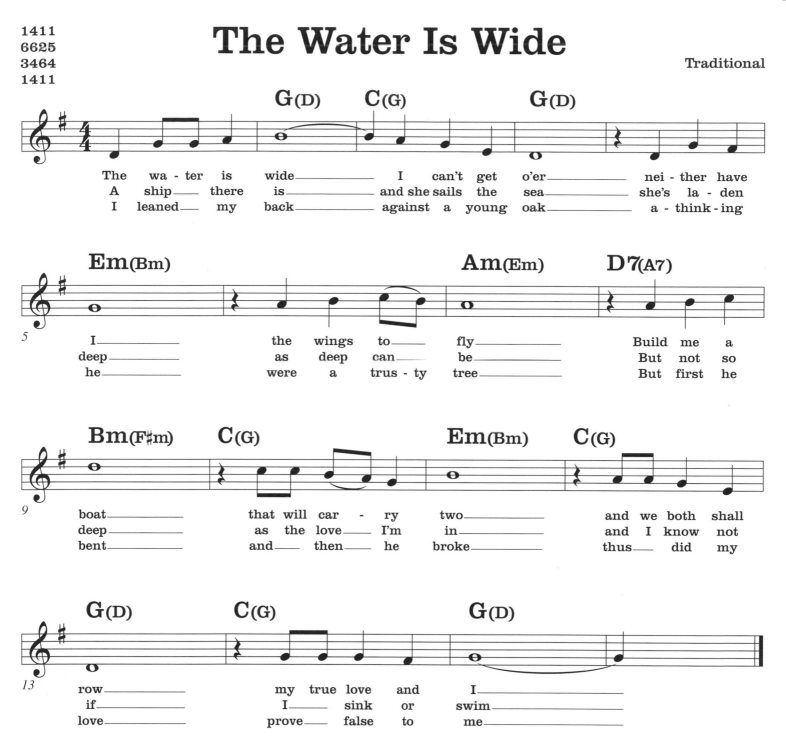

Oh love is handsome, and love is kind
Gay as a jewel, when it's first new
But love grows old, and waxes cold
And fades away like morning dew.

Old Town School of Folk Music

Waterbound

Traditional

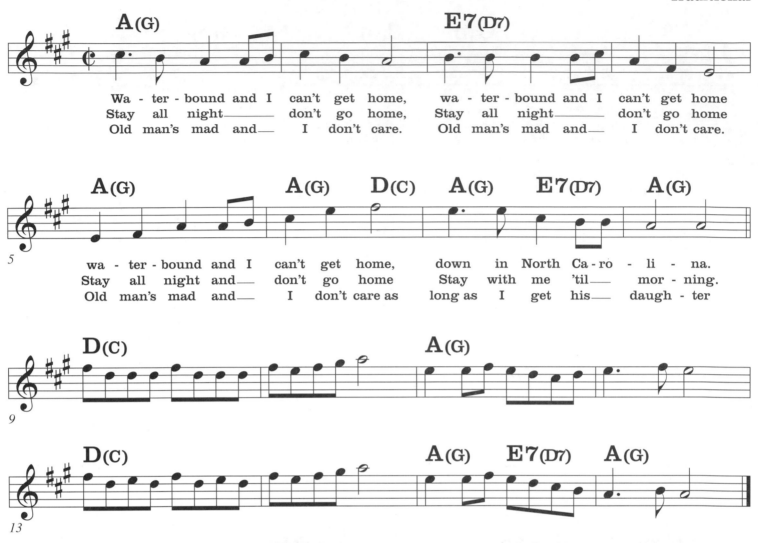

Wa - ter - bound and I can't get home,
wa - ter - bound and I can't get home
Stay all night don't go home,
Stay all night don't go home
Old man's mad and I don't care.
Old man's mad and I don't care.

wa - ter - bound and I can't get home,
down in North Ca - ro - li - na.
Stay all night and don't go home
Stay with me 'til mor - ning.
Old man's mad and I don't care as
long as I get his daugh - ter

Chicken's crowin' in the old corn field
Chicken's crowin' in the old corn field
Chicken's crowin' in the old corn field
Down in North Carolina

Old Town School of Folk Music

Wayfaring Stranger

Traditional

Welcome Table

Traditional

When The Saints Go Marching In

Traditional

1111
1155
1144
1511

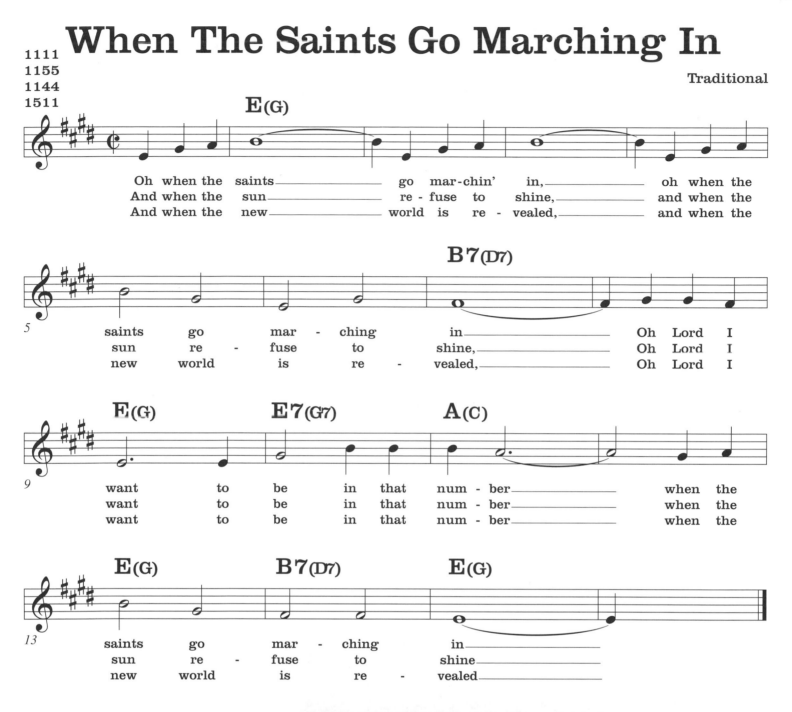

E(G)

Oh when the saints   go mar-chin' in,   oh when the
And when the sun   re - fuse to shine,   and when the
And when the new   world is re - vealed,   and when the

B7(D7)

saints go mar - ching in   Oh Lord I
sun re - fuse to shine,   Oh Lord I
new world is re - vealed,   Oh Lord I

E(G)   **E7(G7)**   **A(C)**

want to be in that num - ber   when the
want to be in that num - ber   when the
want to be in that num - ber   when the

E(G)   **B7(D7)**   **E(G)**

saints go mar - ching in
sun re - fuse to shine
new world is re - vealed

And on that halelujah day
And on that halelujah day
Oh Lord I want to be in that number
On that halelujah day

Old Town School of Folk Music

Wild Mountain Thyme

Traditional

Wild Rover

Traditional

Wildwood Flower

From the Carter Family

1 5-1
1 5-1
1 4-1
1 5-1

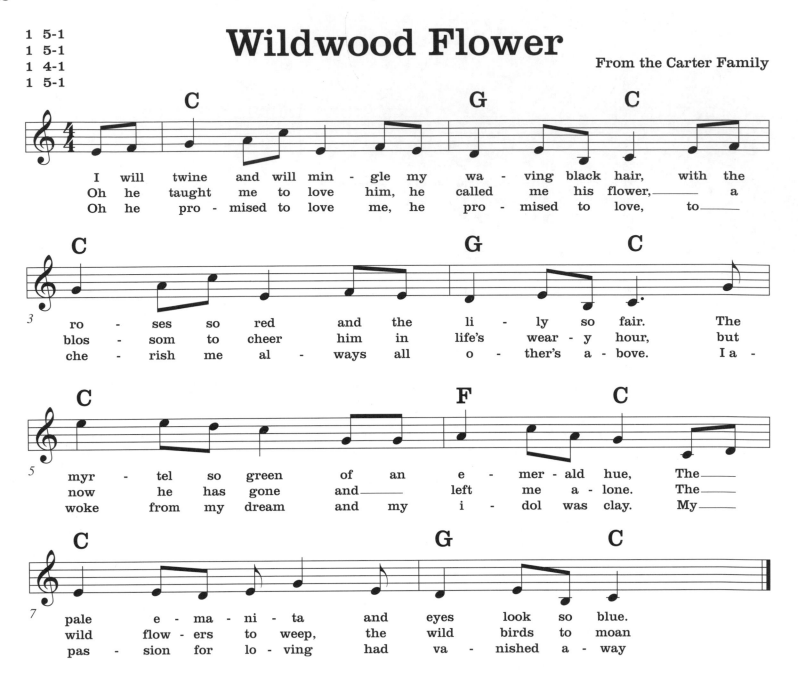

I will twine and will min - gle my wa - ving black hair, with the
Oh he taught me to love him, he called me his flower,_____ a
Oh he pro - mised to love me, he pro - mised to love, to_____

ro - ses so red and the li - ly so fair. The
blos - som to cheer him in life's wear - y hour, but
che - rish me al - ways all o - ther's a - bove. I a -

myr - tel so green of an e - mer - ald hue, The_____
now he has gone and_____ left me a - lone. The_____
woke from my dream and my i - dol was clay. My_____

pale e - ma - ni - ta and eyes look so blue.
wild flow - ers to weep, the wild birds to moan
pas - sion for lo - ving had va - nished a - way

I'll dance and I'll sing and my life shall be gay
I'll charm every heart in the crowd I survey
Though my heart now is breaking, he never shall know
How his name makes me tremble, my pale cheeks to glow

I'll dance and I'll sing and my heart shall be gay
I'll banish this weeping, drive troubles away
I'll live yet to see him regret this dark hour
When he won and neglected this frail wildwood flower

Old Town School of Folk Music

Will The Circle Be Unbroken

Traditional

Wind And Rain

Traditional

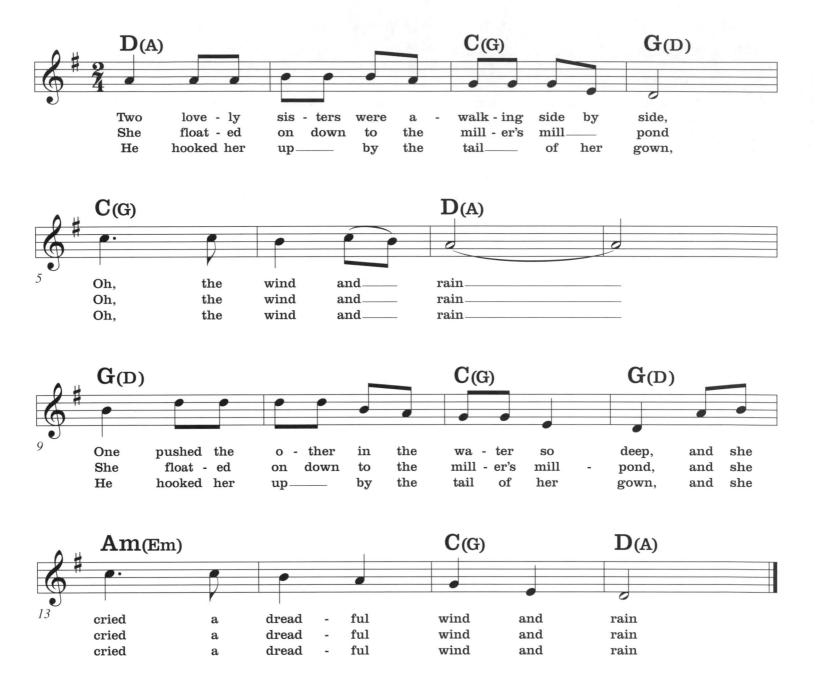

Oh the wind and rain
He made fiddle strings of her long black hair
Oh the wind and rain
He made fiddle strings of her long black hair
And she cried a dreadful wind and rain

He made fiddle screws of her long fingerbones
Oh the wind and rain
He made fiddle screws of her long finger bones
And she cried a dreadful wind and rain

And the only tune that the fiddle would play
Oh the wind and rain
The only tune that fiddle would play
Was oh the dreadful wind and rain

Wings Of An Angel

Lisa DeRosia

CHORUS

Co - ver my heart with the wings of an an - gel
send me to sleep Lord_____ send me to sleep._____ You
can't clip the wings off God's lit - tle an -
gel though the de - vil he creeps_____ de - vil he creeps.

VERSE

Sweet gos - pel mu - sic sings to my soul makes me feel there's
My on - ly heart_____ seems to be break - ing_____ while my
If it's not God_____ that I be - lieve in_____ If it's not

some - place I have left to go. My heart must be show - ing
tongue_____ I'm hol - ding it still, I'll ne - ver for - give the
Je - sus whose sa - ving my soul_____ I'll take my whis-key you

right thru my dress, The blood rush-ing down oh lord what a mess.
things that you've taken, And I'll ne - ver trust the sto - ries you tell.
take your re - li - gion, We'll meet a - gain on the sal - va - tion road.

Old Town School of Folk Music

Worried Man Blues

Traditional

1111
4441
1111
5511

Well I asked the judge, what's gonna be my fine
Well I asked the judge, what's gonna be my fine
Well I asked the judge, what's gonna be my fine
Twenty long years on the R.C. Mountain Line

Old Town School of Folk Music

Old Town School of Folk Music

SOME INSIDE INFORMATION

INDEX

MAJOR, MINOR & DOMINANT CHORDS

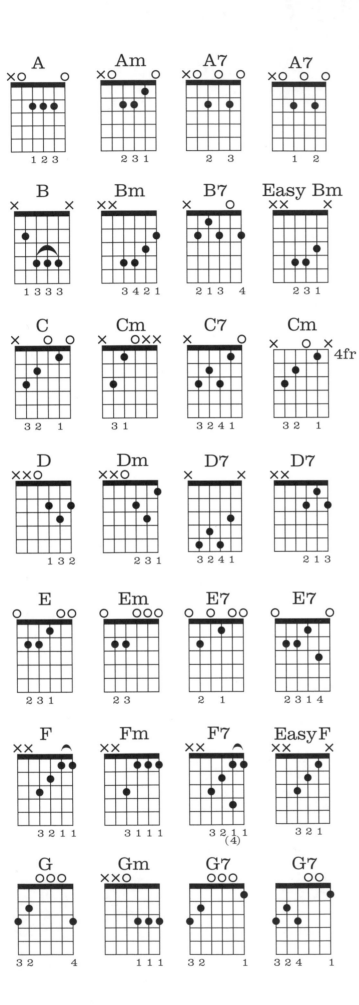

GET THE 145

You'll become a better guitar player if you know the 1, 4 & 5 chords in the keys commonly used by guitar players: C, D, E, G, and A.

Here are those keys

	1	4	5
A	A	D	E
C	C	F	G
D	D	G	A
E	E	A	B
G	G	C	D

MORE GUITAR CHORDS

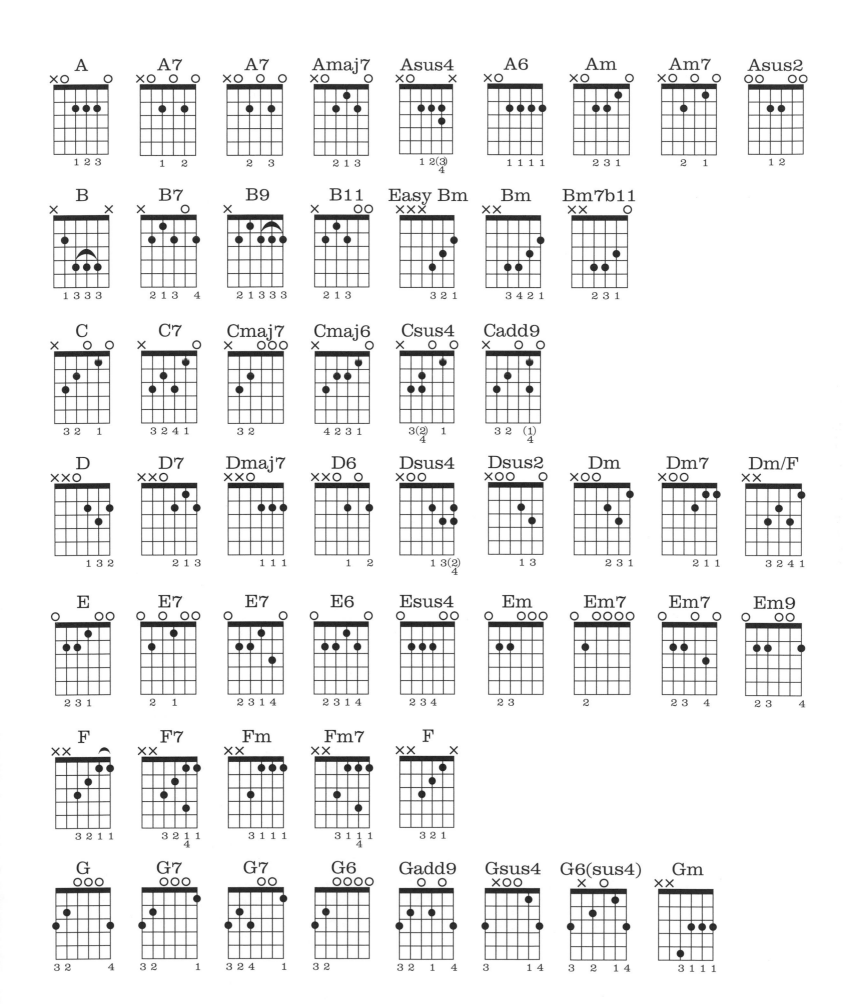

BAR CHORDS

JAZZ CHORDS

ROOT ON THE 5TH STRING

A	A min	A7

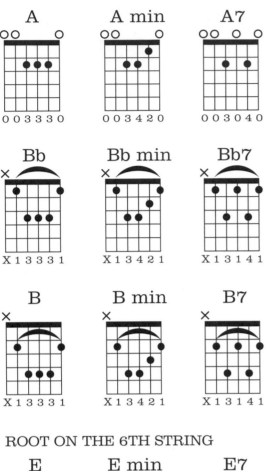

0 0 3 3 3 0   0 0 3 4 2 0   0 0 3 0 4 0

Bb	Bb min	Bb7

X 1 3 3 3 1   X 1 3 4 2 1   X 1 3 1 4 1

B	B min	B7

X 1 3 3 3 1   X 1 3 4 2 1   X 1 3 1 4 1

ROOT ON THE 6TH STRING

E	E min	E7

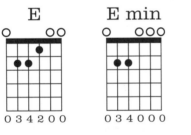

0 3 4 2 0 0   0 3 4 0 0 0   0 3 0 2 0 0

F	F min	F7

1 3 4 2 1 1   1 3 4 1 1 1   1 3 1 2 1 1

F#	F# min	F#7

 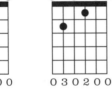 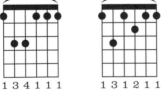 

1 3 4 2 1 1   1 3 4 1 1 1   1 3 1 2 1 1

ROOT ON THE 5TH STRING

Maj7	Maj6	Dom7	Dom9

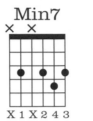 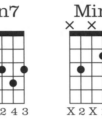 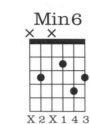 

X 1 3 2 4 X   X 4 2 3 1 X   X 3 2 4 1 X   X 2 1 3 3 3

Min7	Min6	Maj9	Dim7

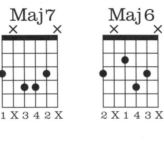  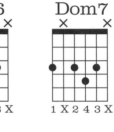  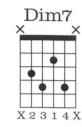

X 1 X 2 4 3   X 2 X 1 4 3   X 2 1 4 3 X   X 2 3 1 4 X

ROOT ON THE 6TH STRING

Maj7	Maj6	Dom7	Dom9

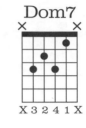 

1 X 3 4 2 X   2 X 1 4 3 X   1 X 2 4 3 X   3 1 4 2 X X

Min7	Min6	Maj9	Dim7

2 X 3 3 3 X   2 X 1 3 3 3   2 X 4 1 3 X   2 X 1 3 1 X

CHORD NAMES: Notice that the bar chords and the jazz chords are listed with "Root on the 6th String," or "Root on the 5th String." These chords have no open strings. Here's a quick reference chart for the names of the notes on the 5th and 6th strings.

FRET	6TH string	5TH string
Open	E	A
1	F	Bb/A#
2	F#/Gb	B
3	G	C
4	G#/Ab	C#/Db
5	A	D
6	A#/Bb	D#/Eb
7	B	E
8	C	F
9	C#/Db	F#/Gb
10	D	G
11	D#/Eb	G#/Ab
12	E	A

138

OPEN G TUNING CHORDS (DGDGBD)

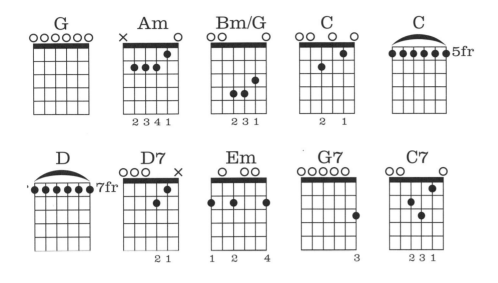

OPEN D TUNING CHORDS (DADF#AD)

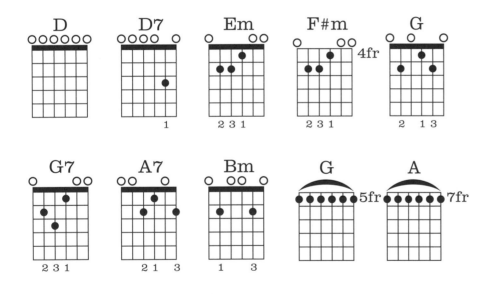

HOW TO TUNE THE GUITAR

Here are five different ways to check the tuning of your guitar. Many guitarists use multiple methods of tuning to verify if the instrument is in tune.

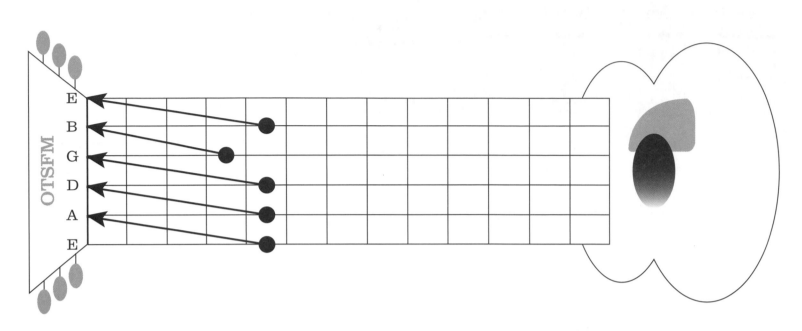

#1: RELATIVE TUNING

Use this chart to learn the names and number of the strings and how to tune the strings in relation to one another.

1st string E = 2nd string B @ 5th fret
2nd string B = 3rd string G @ 4th fret
3rd string G = 4th string D @ 5th fret
4th string D = 5th string A @ 5th fret
5th string A = 6th string E @ 5th fret

#2: TUNING BY OCTAVES

An octave is an interval of 12 half steps. Consider the melody line of the scale do, re, mi, fa, so, la, ti, do the first and the last do are one octave apart. There are a series of octave relationships among that strings that are useful for tuning.

Notes & Locations For Octaves

E	6/0	4/2	1/0
A	5/0	3/2	
D	4/0	2/3	
G	3/0	1/3	

#3: TUNING BY HARMONICS

Harmonics are chime-like sounds that are created at set locations on the strings. Matching harmonics sounds is another way to tune.

Play them this way:

Left hand lightly touches the string directly over the fret. Do not push down on the string.

Right hand plays the string close to the bridge. It helps to hit the string with conviction to get a good harmonic sound.

The chart below lists the note name, the harmonic location, and location for fundamental pitch.

Notes & Locations For Harmonics

Note	Harm	Harm	Fund
E	6/5	5/7	open 1
A	5/5	4/7	1/5
D	4/5	3/7	1/10
B	2/5	1/7	1/19

#4: TUNING BY INTERVALS

Tuning by intervals means learning to recognize the relationships among the sounds of the open strings. The interval between string 6 and string 5 is called a perfect 4th. The chart below shows the intervals of all adjacent strings.

Mnemonic devices come in handy when trying to learn intervals.
The first two notes of:
"Here Come the Bride" = a perfect 4th
"Oh When The Saints" = a major 3rd

Notes & Locations For Intervals

Num/Name	Num/Name	INT	Tune
6-E	5-A	Perfect 4th	"Bride"
5-A	4-D	Perfect 4th	"Bride"
4-D	3-G	Perfect 4th	"Bride"
3-G	2-B	Major 3rd	"Saints"
2-B	1-E	Perfect 4th	"Bride"

#5: TUNING BY CHORDS

Strum a few chords on your guitar and listen carefully. Sometimes a string that sounds in tune when the string is played open, does not sound in tune when fretted and may need some slight adjustment.

CONCERT PITCH AND TUNING FORKS

All of these tuning methods assume that you're in "concert pitch." That means that the note A = 440 Hz and that if you play an A note on the guitar, it will be the same frequency as an A note on the piano. The most accurate way to get concert pitch starting notes is with a tuning fork. An A440 tuning fork will give you the A note at 1/5; or the harmonic at 5/5 or 4/7.

AUTOMATIC TUNERS

Get one. They're not too expensive, and having a tuner is like having insurance. Having your guitar in tune will help develop your ear.

CHROMATIC SCALE

All notes have names within the musical alphabet of A through G. Below is the guitar neck with the names of all the notes.

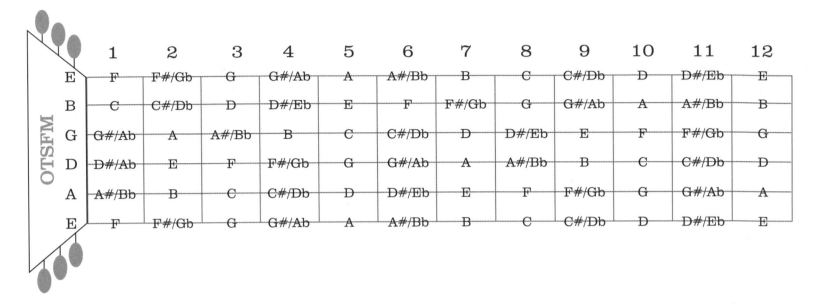

	1	2	3	4	5	6	7	8	9	10	11	12
E	F	F#/Gb	G	G#/Ab	A	A#/Bb	B	C	C#/Db	D	D#/Eb	E
B	C	C#/Db	D	D#/Eb	E	F	F#/Gb	G	G#/Ab	A	A#/Bb	B
G	G#/Ab	A	A#/Bb	B	C	C#/Db	D	D#/Eb	E	F	F#/Gb	G
D	D#/Ab	E	F	F#/Gb	G	G#/Ab	A	A#/Bb	B	C	C#/Db	D
A	A#/Bb	B	C	C#/Db	D	D#/Eb	E	F	F#/Gb	G	G#/Ab	A
E	F	F#/Gb	G	G#/Ab	A	A#/Bb	B	C	C#/Db	D	D#/Eb	E

There are a few things that are helpful to notice about this diagram.

1. Remember from tuning that you fret the 5th fret of the lowest string to get the pitch for its adjacent open string. They are the same notes with the same names (6th string/5th fret = A and the open 5th string = A).
2. Sharps (#) and Flats (b)
   *Sharp, indicated by the symbol (#) means higher in pitch by one fret (one half step).
   *Flat, indicated by the symbol (b) means lower in pitch by one fret (one half step).
3. The musical alphabet goes from A to G, no farther.
4. Some notes have two names. For example, the note between F and G is called either F# or Gb, depending on the key being played.
5. Notice that there are no flats or sharps between B-C or between E-F.
   These are called natural half steps.

SUGGESTED EXERCISES

To get a better sense of these principles, try the following exercises:

1. Find every G note on the neck of the guitar up to the 12th fret.
   (Hint: There is at least one on every string.)
2. Play the chromatic scale on a single string and say the name of the note as you play it.
3. Place your finger at any point on the neck. Let that note that you play be the first note to the tune "Happy Birthday." See if you can figure out the melody using the hunt and peck method.
4. Finger the chords that you know how to play on the guitar and find the names to the notes you are playing. For example, what note does your index finger play in a D Major chord?

TRANSPOSITION, CHORDS, & CAPOS

Here's a chart of most of the keys in music and the diatonic chords in those keys.

	I	ii	iii	IV	V	vi	vii	bVII
	1	2	3	4	5	6	7	b7
A	A	Bm	C#m	D	E	F#m	G#dim	G7
Bb	Bb	Cm	Dm	Eb	F	Gm	Adim	Ab7
B	B	C#m	D#m	E	F#	G#m	A#dim	A7
C	D	Dm	Em	F	G	Am	Bdim	Bb7
Db	Db	Ebm	Fm	Gb	Ab	Bbm	Cdim	B7
D	D	Em	F#m	G	A	Bm	C#dim	C7
Eb	Eb	Fm	Gm	Ab	Bb	Cm	Ddim	Db7
E	E	F#m	G#m	A	B	C#m	D#dim	D7
F	F	Cm	Am	Bb	C	Dm	Edim	Eb7
Gb	Gb	Abm	Bbm	Cb	Db	Ebm	Fdim	E7
G	G	Am	Bm	C	D	Em	F#dim	F7
Ab	Ab	Bbm	Cm	Db	Eb	Fm	Gdim	Gb7

WHAT DO THE NUMBERS MEAN?

1. Songs are written in keys, following the musical alphabet, which runs from A through G.
2. The numbers refer to scale degrees based on Do, Re, Mi.
3. The numbers also correspond to chord types.
   - Major chords are built on scale degrees 1, 4, and 5.
   - Minor chords are built on scale degrees 2, 3, and 6.
   - Diminished chord is built on scale degree 7.
   - Scale degrees 1 and 8 are the same note, one octave apart.

HOW TO USE THE TRANSPOSITION CHART

Transposition means changing a song from one key to another. This chart will help you do that.

Follow these steps:

1. Identify the key you are in.
   (For example, the key of C)

2. Choose the key you want to go to.
   (For example, the key of A)

3. Substitute the new chords.

Scale	Degree	Chord
Do	1	Major
Re	2	Minor
Mi	3	Minor
Fa	4	Major
So	5	Major
La	6	Minor
Ti	7	Dim
Do	8	

C	to	A
G	to	E
Am	to	F#m
Bdim	to	G#dim
Bb7	to	G7

TRANSPOSITION, CHORDS, & CAPOS (con't)

GET THE 1, 4, 5

You'll become a better guitar player if you know the 1, 4 and 5 chords in the keys commonly used by guitar players: C, D, E, G and A.

Here are those keys:

	1	4	5
A	A	D	E
C	C	F	G
D	D	G	A
E	E	A	B
G	G	C	D

An easy way to find and remember the 1, 4, 5 chords in these common guitar keys is to count on your fingers up the musical alphabet from A to G. For example, if C is one, go up four letters and there is F; go up five letters and there is G.

CAPOS AND HOW THEY WORK

Capos allows a player to use familiar fingerings while changing keys.

Whatever fret you put the capo on raises the pitch of your chord by as many half steps. For example, put a capo at the 2nd fret and play a C chord. The C chord now sounds as a D, two half steps higher. Put the capo at the 3rd fret and play it again. The C chord now sounds as D# or Eb, three half steps higher, etc.

HOW TO USE THE CAPO CHART

Use this chart to discover the most common ways that guitarists achieve different sounds up and down the neck.

ORIENTATION DEFINED

We use the term "orientation" to indicate a set of chord shapes associated with a specific key. For example, playing in the key of A, a guitarist gets accustomed to playing the 1, 4 and 5 chords which are A, D and E. That is called an "A orientation."

For Example: Key of C
1. Play C, F and G7 with no capo.
2. Put capo at 3 and play A, D and E7. Even though you are playing with an "A orientation," your guitar is sounding in the key of C because of the capo.
3. Put capo at 5 and play in the G orientation using G, C and D7.
4. Put capo at 8 and play in an E orientation using E, A and B7.
5. In each of the these examples, playing all these different chords, you are actually playing in the key of C.

KEY	1, 4, 5 chords		
C	**C, F, G7**	**New Shape**	**New Chords**
	Capo at 3	A orientation	A, D, E7
	Capo at 5	G orientation	G, C, D7
	Capo at 8	E orientation	E, A, B7

KEY	1, 4, 5 chords		
D	**D, G, A7**	**New Shape**	**New Chords**
	Capo at 2	C orientation	C, F, G7
	Capo at 5	A orientation	A, D, E7
	Capo at 7	G orientation	G, C, D7

KEY	1, 4, 5 chords		
E	**E, A, B7**	**New Shape**	**New Chords**
	Capo at 2	D orientation	D, G A7
	Capo at 4	C orientation	C, F, G7
	Capo at 7	A orientation	A, D, E7

KEY	1, 4, 5 chords		
F	**F, Bb, C7**	**New Shape**	**New Chords**
	Capo at 1	E orientation	E, A, B7
	Capo at 3	D orientation	D, G A7
	Capo at 5	C orientation	C, F, G7
	Capo at 8	A orientation	A, D, E7

KEY	1, 4, 5 chords		
G	**G, C, D7**	**New Shape**	**New Chords**
	Capo at 3	E orientation	E, A, B7
	Capo at 5	D orientation	D, G A7
	Capo at 7	C orientation	C, F, G7

KEY	1, 4, 5 chords		
A	**A, D, E7**	**New Shape**	**New Chords**
	Capo at 2	G orientation	G, C, D7
	Capo at 5	E orientation	E, A, B7
	Capo at 7	D orientation	D, G, A7
	Capo at 9	C orientation	C, F, G7

KEY	1, 4, 5 chords		
Bb	**Bb, Eb, F7**	**New Shape**	**New Chords**
	Capo at 1	A orientation	A, D, E7
	Capo at 3	G orientation	G, C, D7
	Capo at 6	E orientation	E, A, B7
	Capo at 8	D orientation	D, G, A7

KEY	1, 4, 5 chords		
Eb	**Eb, Ab, Bb7**	**New Shape**	**New Chords**
	Capo at 1	D orientation	D, G, A7
	Capo at 3	C orientation	C, F, G7
	Capo at 6	A orientation	A, D, E7
	Capo at 8	G orientation	G, C, D7

Circle of 5th's

HOW TO READ TABLATURE

Tablature indicates where and when to play a note on a fretted instrument.

FRACTION TAB: Written as a fraction string/fret. This might be used to write a simple bass line.

6 LINE GUITAR TAB: Written where the six lines of the staff refer to the six strings of the guitar, and the numbers refer to the fret.

EXAMPLE 1: Fraction Tab

Read this as string/fret

5/3 4/2 3/0 2/1

NOTE BY NOTE

5/3 = 5th string at the 3rd fret

4/2 = 4th string at the 2nd fret

3/0 = 3rd string open

2/1 = 2nd string at the 1st fret

EXAMPLE 2: Six-line Tablature

Here the lines are the strings, the numbers are the frets.

NOTE BY NOTE

5th string at the 3rd fret

4th string at the 2nd fret

3rd string open

2nd string at the 1st fret

You may recognize this as the notes of a C chord.

EXAMPLE 3: Tablature with RH fingering

This example uses the PIMA abbreviations for the right hand.

P = thumb, I = index finger

M = middle finger, A = ring finger

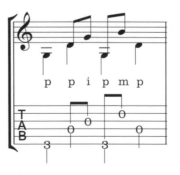

NOTE BY NOTE

6/3 played by RH thumb (p)

4/0 played by RH thumb (p)

3/0 played by RH index finger (i)

6/3 played by RH thumb (p)

2/0 played by RH middle finger (m)

4/0 played by RH thumb (p)

SCALES

All melodies are built on scales. There are many. Here are just a few to try.

MAJOR SCALES, ONE STRING

This is the same as Do Re Mi Fa So La Ti Do.
It follows the magic phone number 221-2221
Try it on any open string.

G SCALE, ONE OCTAVE

Try it in the 1st position* with the index finger at
1st fret, middle finger at 2nd fret, and ring finger
at 3rd fret.

*Position means where your index finger is, with the implication of
one finger per fret thereafter. Index finger @ 1 middle finger @ 2 ring
finger @ 3 and pinky @ 4.

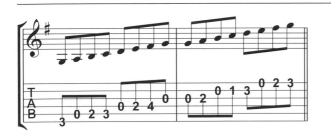

G SCALE, TWO OCTAVES

Try it in the 1st position* starting with ring
finger at 6/3.

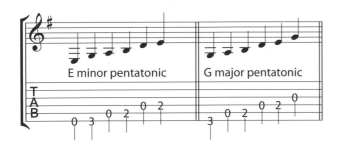

PENTATONIC SCALES

These are five-note scales. Notice that the E minor
and G Major pentatonic scale are comprised of the
same notes, with different starting points.

Scale Degrees Are:
Minor: R-b3-4-5-b7-R
Major: R-2-3-5-6-R

BLUES SCALES

This is a modified pentatonic scale with a b5
note added. Here is the E blues scale written in
two different locations.

Scale Degrees Are:
R-b3-4-b5-5-b7

HARMONIZED SCALES

Harmony happens when two notes are played together. Here are four harmonized scales based on the notes of the C and G scales.

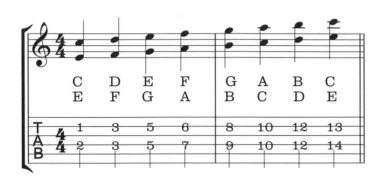

KEY OF C: 6TH below the root

C scale harmonized by starting on the note E, a 6th of the scale, below the root.

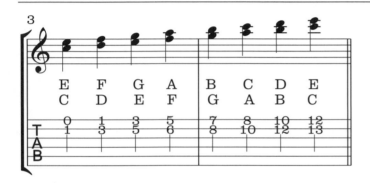

KEY OF C: 3RD above the root

C scale harmonized by starting on the note E, a 3rd of the scale above the root.

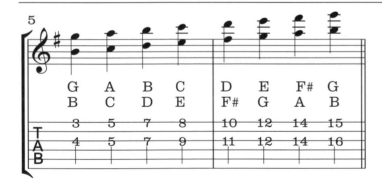

KEY OF G: 6TH below the root

G scale harmonized by starting on the note B, a 6th of the scale, below the root.

KEY OF G: 3rd above the root

G scale harmonized by starting on the note B, a 3rd of the scale, above the root.

ARPEGGIOS & FINGERPICKING

1. Arpeggio picking plays one chord tone at a time.

2. Travis Picking (aka alternate thumb picking) is where the thumb plays an alternating bass pattern that drives the song forward.

3. Right hand fingering will be indicated using PIMA method.
P = thumb I = index finger
M = middle finger A = ring finger

4. Anarchy is tradition. These are recommendations, not rules.

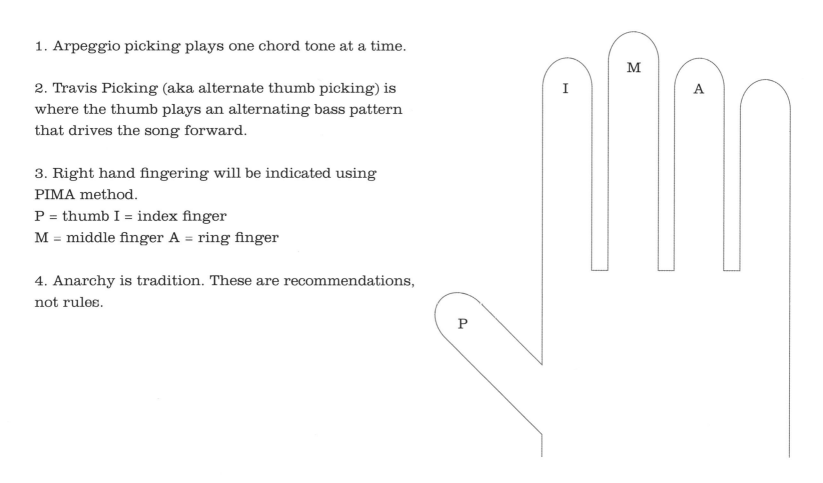

ARPEGGIOSs with open strings. P = thumb I = index finger M = middle finger A = ring finger.

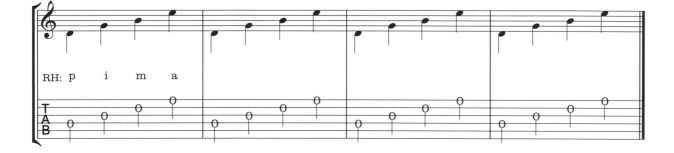

ARPEGGIOS through a simple chord progression.

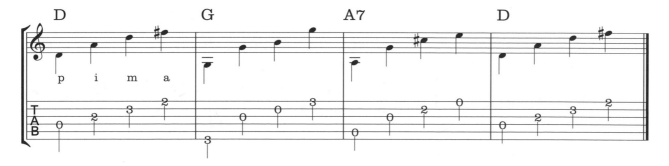

TRAVIS PICKING

Named after renowned guitarist, Merle Travis, and deeply rooted in fingerstyle blues, this style of guitar is heard throughout American music.

TIP #1: Play through the thumb exercises. They create the foundation for Travis picking.
TIP #2: The Travis patterns are all on open strings. Try them with different chords.

THUMB EXERCISES
TIP: The thumb is the fingerpicking rhythm section. Fingerpicking, especially Travis style, depends entirely on the driving rhythm of the thumb.

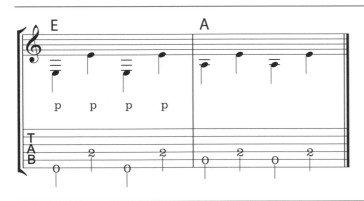

ALTERNATING BASS (thumb only)
ON OPEN STRINGS.

TIP: Make sure to keep an even beat.

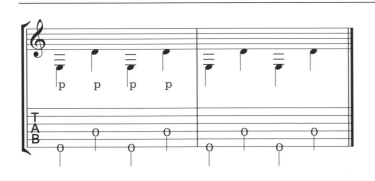

ALTERNATING BASS (thumb only)
MOVING FROM E TO A
TIP: E chord alternates between 6 & 4.
A chord alternates between 5 & 4.

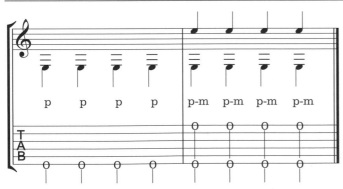

PINCHING EXERCISE
TIP: Play 6th string with thumb (P) and 1st string with middle finger (M)

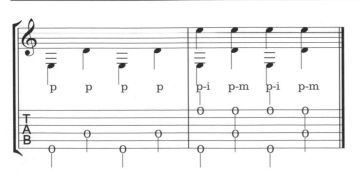

PINCHING EXERCISE WITH
ALTERNATING BASS
TIP: Try to follow the right hand (PIMA) suggestions.

TRAVIS PATTERNS

Here are four samples of Travis picking patterns. There are dozens. What they have in common is the steady driving thumb.

TIP: What your thumb does is mandatory, what your fingers do is arbitrary.

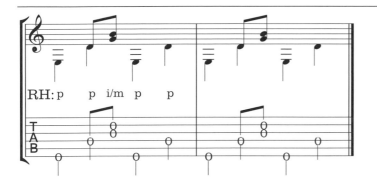

TRAVIS PATTERN #1

TIP: Fingers only play between 2nd and 3rd beat.

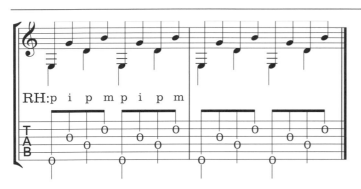

TRAVIS PATTERN #2

TIP: Every other note is played with your thumb.

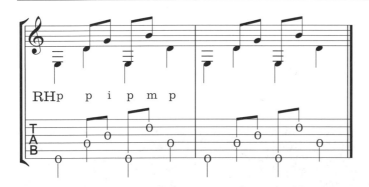

TRAVIS PATTERN #3

TIP: Very similar to #2 but with two fewer notes.

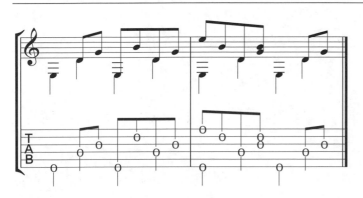

TRAVIS PATTERN VARIATIONS

TIP: With the same steady thumb in the bass there are dozens of variations to explore.

NASHVILLE NUMBERS AND CHORD CHARTS

Many of the songs in this book have a chord chart summary in the upper left hand corner of the page, indicating the chord progression for any key. For example, look at Aunt Rhody. Notice that in the upper left hand corner you see this:

1 1 5 1
1 1 5 1

From this you know:

1. Chord progression is 8 measures long.
2. You play two measures of the 1 chord, one measure of the 5 chord, and one measure of the 1 chord. And then you repeat that. And that's the whole song.

In the key of D, it would be this:

D D A D
D D A D

In the key of C, it would be:

C C G C
C C G C

THE 5 CHORD IS DOMINANT

In most songs the 5 chord can be played as a Dominant 7.

TRY THIS

Play the chord progression to "Aunt Rhody" in the key of D using an A Major chord. Now try the same chord progression using an A7 chord. Use the one you like best, but know that they are interchangeable. Explore the sound of playing the 5 chord in other songs as both a major chord, or a Dominant 7th.

I, IV, V vs 1, 4, 5

In most written forms, Roman numerals are used to indicate the chord numbers I, IV, and V. For simplicity, we have used the Arabic numbers 1, 4, and 5 because they sound the same.

ALTERED HARMONY

In some songs, the minor chords are played as major. For example look at "Freight Train," p. 46. It is in the key of C. In the key of C, the 3 chord would be E minor, but in "Freight Train" it is E^7, a major chord. This is indicated by underlining the 3.

BANJO

Right Hand Abbreviations are different from the guitar.

T = thumb; I = index finger; M = middle finger; Pinch = TIM together; Brush = strum with M

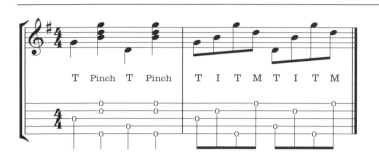

FINGERPICKING ACCOMPANIMENT

Try these patterns. No fingerpicks necessary. Play through a few chords.

BLUEGRASS: FORWARD ROLL

Earl Scruggs revolutionized the banjo with his electrifying and syncopated banjo playing. The forward roll is at the foundation of the sound.

BLUEGRASS: BACKWARD ROLL

The perfect compliment to the forward roll is the backward roll. The artistry is in the combination of sounds like these.

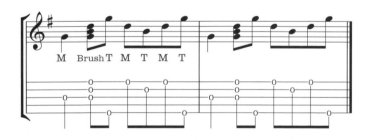

FRAILING (aka Clawhammer Banjo)

This is an ancient way of playing strings, dating back hundreds of years to northern and western Africa. This style features a downward attack on the strings. Contact is made with nail of the middle finger hitting down on single strings or strumming.

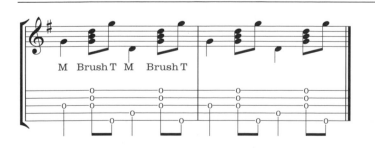

FRAILING: Double Thumbing Technique

This technique, common among frailers, is where the thumb comes off the 5th string and plays any other. For best results, make sure your thumb is resting on the string before it plays it.

HARMONICA

THE D HARMONICA

The **top row** are notes you get by releasing air into the harp ('blowing')

The **lower row** are notes you get by lightly pulling air back through the harp ('drawing')

HOLES	1	2	3	4	5	6	7	8	9	10
	D	F#	A	D	F#	A	D	F#	A	D
	E	A	C#	E	G	B	C#	E	G	B

JUST DO IT!

Probably the best thing to do is just get a harmonica, purse your lips to make a little oval opening in the middle, and start trying to play any song. You'll find that some notes are there and some are not.

STRAIGHT HARP FOR FOLK SONGS; CROSS HARP FOR BLUES

If you want to play a folk song in a major key, like "Oh Susanah," it is best to have a harmonica in that key. That is playing "straight harp." If you want to play blues, like "When Things Go Wrong with You, It Hurts Me Too" most people play "cross harp." That means that they choose a harp that is a 4th above the key of that song. To play blues in A, you use a harp in D. For blues in C, you play an F harp. For blues in E, play an A harp. This approach uses more "draw" (air coming in) notes; after you play more, that's where you'll find the best blues notes.

MANY POSSIBILITIES

You can play in a number of keys on any diatonic harmonica. Below are some important "starting places" for chords and melody on any harp. Key fact: The starting melody note of any song is likely to be a note right there in the chord played with that melody!

PARTIAL CHORDS ON THE 'G' and 'D' HARMONICAS (HARMONICA I)

Underlined numbers mean DRAW; Not underlined means BLOW

Song is in	Type of song	Harp	I chord	IV chord	V chord
Key of G	Country, simple melody	G Harp	G = 56 or any blow	C = 56	D = 45
	Blues or heavy rhythm	C Harp	G = 123	C = 123 or any blow	D = 4 or 1 - 4*
	Swing, other	D Harp	G = 56	D = 45	D = 56
Key of D	Country, simple melody	D Harp	D = 56 or any blow	G = 56	A = 45
	Blues or heavy rhythm	G Harp	D = 123	G = 123 or any blow	A = 4 1 - 4*
	Swing, other	A Harp	D = 56	G = 45	A = 56

BANJO CHORDS (G tuning: gDGBD)

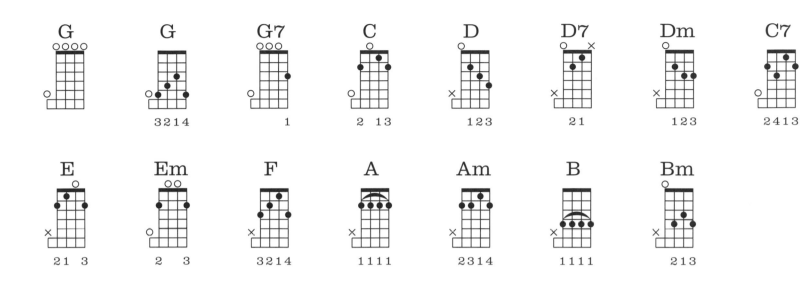

UKULELE CHORDS (tuning: GCEA)

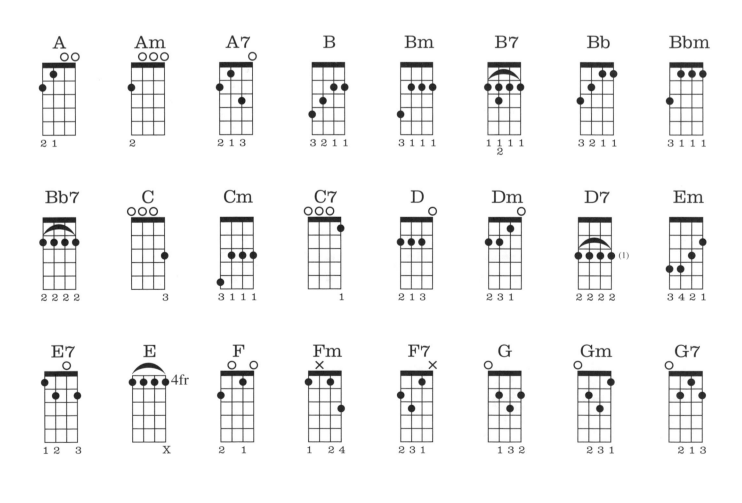

156

DULCIMER CHORDS (tuning: DAD)

Chords: I | IV | V | ii | iii | vi
D | G | A7 | Em | F#m | Bm

nut
1
2
3
4
5
6+
7

MANDOLIN CHORDS (tuning: GDAE)

A | A7 | Am | B | B7 | Bm | Bb | C

C7 | Cm | D | D7 | Dm | E | E7 | Em

F | G | G7 | Gm

TAB CHARTS

CHORD CHARTS

NOTES

OLD TOWN SCHOOL OF FOLK MUSIC

MISSION: Old Town School of Folk Music teaches and celebrates music and cultural expressions rooted in the traditions of diverse American and global communities.

Old Town School of Folk Music has grown to become one of the largest independent community arts schools in the United States. Yet despite its size and presence, the intensely social, intimate and uncomplicated atmosphere of the Old Town School is as accessible and important as it was in 1957.

Every week, a few at a time, students and teaching artists gather to study and share their passions for music and the arts together. All in all, several hundred thousand students of all ages have taken part in these highly personal encounters. Whatever one's interest, the Old Town School provides broad access to group classes, private lessons, and workshops that span a wide range of artistic genres. Old Town School's critically acclaimed concerts and special events showcase a diverse array of local, national and international artists, and strive to make the arts available to all with a wide range of free and low cost performances.

Old Town School of Folk Music provides nationally accredited classes in music, dance, theater, and visual arts to people of all ages, abilities, and backgrounds. Old Town School education programs are accredited by the Accrediting Commission for Community & Precollegiate Arts Schools. The Old Town School is one of only a handful of community arts schools in the nation with accredited status and the only one devoted to teaching traditional and popular art forms from around the world.

DEDICATED to our students - past, present, and future - for deciding to make music an important part of their lives.

ACKNOWLEDGEMENTS for assistance and direction on this book: Keith Baumann, Dona Benkert, Mark Dvorak, Ben Harbert, Margaret James, Charles Kim, Skip Landt, C. Lanialoha Lee, Steve Levitt, Colby Maddox, Bob Medich, Michael Miles, Elaine Moore, Krista Ortgiesen, Kerry Sheehan, Jacob Sweet, Jimmy Tomasello, Christopher Walz, and the many staff and faculty members who have inspired us with their support and dedication.